Physical Characteristics of the Maltese

(from the American Kennel Club breed standard)

Body: Compact, the height from the withers to the ground equaling the length from the withers to the root of the tail. Shoulder blades are sloping, the elbows well knit and held close to the body. The back is level in topline, the ribs well sprung. The chest is fairly deep, the loins taut, strong, and just slightly tucked up underneath.

Tail: A long-haired plume carried gracefully over the back, its tip lying to the side over the quarter.

Coat and Color: The coat is single, that is, without undercoat. It hangs long, flat, and silky over the sides of the body almost, if not quite, to the ground. Color, pure white.

Size: Weight under 7 pounds, with from 4 to 6 pounds preferred.

Maltese

◇

By Juliette Cunliffe

Contents

Maltese

by Charlotte Schwartz
Be informed about the importance of training your Maltese
from the basics of housebreaking and understanding the development of a young dog to executing obedience commands (sit,
stay, down, etc.).

Discover how to select a qualified veterinarian and care for
your dog at all stages of life. Topics include vaccination scheduling, skin problems, dealing with external and internal parasites
and common medical and behavioral conditions.

Experience the dog show world, including different types of
shows and the making of a champion. Go beyond the conformation ring to other pursuits for your Maltese.

KENNEL CLUB BOOKS: MALTESE
ISBN: 1-59378-251-9

Copyright © 1999 • **Revised American Edition: Copyright © 2003**
Kennel Club Books, Inc., 308 Main Street, Allenhurst, NJ 07711 USA
Cover Design Patented: US 6,435,559 B2 • Printed in South Korea

PHOTO CREDITS:
Photos by Isabelle Français, with additional photos provided by:
Norvia Behling, T.J. Calhoun, Carolina Biological Supply, Doskocil, James Hayden-Yoav,
James R. Hayden, RBP, Bill Jonas, Carol Ann Johnson, Dwight R. Kuhn,
Dr. Dennis Kunkel, Mikki Pet Products, Antonio Philippe, Phototake,
Jean Claude Revy and Dr. Andrew Spielman.
Illustrations by Patricia Peters.

The publisher wishes to thank Kathleen Bakeman, Emanuel Cominiti, Claudia Grunstra, Linda Johnson,
Johane Kriegel, Robin Lindemann, Beverly A. Nucci, Beverly Quilliam, Nancy Roberts, Christopher Vicari
and the rest of the owners of dogs featured in this book.

The Maltese has been favored for thousands of years. It was the European answer to Oriental lapdogs. Sailors and explorers brought back tales of tiny dogs that fit into the large sleeves or sat in the laps of the aristocrat Chinese, presumably to keep their owners warm!

MALTESE

The Maltese is almost undoubtedly one of the most ancient lap dogs of the Western World, but there has long been dispute over the actual origin of this charming breed. Charles Darwin placed the breed as having existed around 6000 BC, although a model of such a dog, some 2,000 years older, has since been found. This is presumed to have been a child's toy. The Emperor Claudius (10 BC–AD 54) had such a dog, and it seems likely that they were taken to Asia by the Romans. Eventually they reached China, where it is believed that dogs of Maltese type contributed to the ancestral breeding of the Pekingese dog known today.

The breed has had numerous names during the course of history, including "Melitae Dog," "Ye Ancient Dogge of Malta," "Comforter," "Spaniel Gentle," "Shock Dog" and "Maltese Lion Dog." The latter name most probably alludes to the fact that several of the early toy breeds had their coats styled into a "lion trim." This caused some confusion among the breeds, especially with the breed now known for this cut, called the Löwchen (Little Lion Dog).

Many pre-Christian objects of art are adorned with the image of

the Maltese, and in the courts of Imperial Rome, the Maltese was a favorite among the ladies, once being known as the "Roman Ladies' Dog." It was written of these dogs, "When his favorite dies he deposits the remains in a tomb and erects a monument over the grave with the inscription, 'Offspring of the stock of Malta'." Certainly Maltese were closely involved in Egyptian culture between 600 and 300 BC, at which time they were effectively worshipped as members of royal families.

In Greece, the first known written history of the breed was recorded around 350 BC by the philosopher-poet Aristotle, who attributed the origin of the breed to Malta, in the Mediterranean Sea. However, images of the Maltese have been found on Greek vases dating back to 500 BC.

Many of the early Italian painters included dogs in their paintings, and these dogs appear to have been Maltese. To throw further confusion upon the geographic origin of the breed, in AD 25 there was a town in Sicily called Melitia. Here beautiful little dogs called *Canis Melitei* were found. Confusion understandably could have arisen because the island of Malta was earlier known as the Island of Melita. Writing in 1851, Youatt tells us that they were found not only in Malta but in other islands of the Mediterranean, where they "maintained the same character of being devotedly affectionate to their owners...[but] ill-tempered to strangers." Although he said they were no bigger than common ferrets or weasels, he considered them "not small in understanding nor unstable in their love."

Some consider that the Maltese was one of the original French toy breeds, and it is certainly a close relation of bichon breeds such as the Bichon Frise, Bolognese and Havanese, and the Coton de Tuléar. However, the Maltese should not be confused with today's Bichon Frise, despite the fact that at certain points in its history it has actually been called "Bichon." Some breeders have even thought that the breed actually hails from the Gobi Desert, something that was attributed to their love of heat and sun.

THE MALTESE USED FOR TRADE

The Maltese's place of origin becomes further confused by the fact that this dog traveled extensively to different parts of the world, being used in trade as barter for Chinese silk, among other

The Maltese Terrier known as Eng. Ch. Pixie was owned by Joshua Jacobs circa 1900.

things. Silk at that time was indeed precious, and in weight it was considered as valuable as gold. According to the writer Idstone, Maltese were often taken to the shore for sale, or else the owners of shore boats held them up to the passengers. Sadly he added that they were "simply long-haired little wretches, washed, starched and combed out…"

THE MALTESE TERRIER?

In more recent years, the Maltese has been known as the "Maltese Terrier," but it is generally believed that the early makeup of the breed lay in dogs of spitz or spaniel type, rather than those of terrier type. Having said that, though, the character of the breed certainly made the dogs eminently capable of catching a mouse or a rat. During the breed's early years, there is evidence that it was used as a small hunting dog, although it was then much larger than the breed we know today.

MALTESE LORE

The Maltese has long captured the affection of man, and many a book included vivid anecdotal images about the breed. The list is endless, including a story about one Maltese that threw himself into his master's grave, another that climbed upon a funeral pyre and one that even reputedly climbed onto the gallows.

Mrs. Stallibrass with her Maltese Terrier, Queen Stallie. Mrs. Stallibrass was one of the breed's most staunch supporters at the turn of the 20th century in England.

GERMAN THOUGHTS ON THE BREED

In 1650, a German physician stated that a toothache could be cured by scraping one's gums with a dog's tooth, and then went on to describe the Maltese dog at some length. He believed that the breed had originated in Malta and talked of two varieties, one with short hair, the other with long, flowing hair. He described them as being the size of a wood weasel and said that at that time red and white dogs were most valued, although he also mentioned that there had been black and white ones. To ensure that Maltese dogs would maintain their small size, they were shut up in baskets in which they were fed, but their food was of the choicest kind and their beds were lined with fleeces.

Although it is not known when the Maltese actually arrived in Germany, they were certainly in the country by 1860 and were exhibited at shows there from 1879. A German Stud Book was established in 1900, and from this point onward dog breeding was taken very seriously, leading to the formation of the Lapdog Club of Berlin in 1902. Just two years later, a breed standard was issued in Germany for the Maltese, followed by a Toy Breeds Register in 1910.

THE MALTESE COMES TO BRITAIN

In 1859, a lady by the name of Miss Gibbs obtained a little bitch, Psyche, from a gentleman who had obtained her from his brother, a ship's captain. Psyche was pure white and was reputed to have looked like "a ball of animated floss." The hair on her shoulders was 15 ins. long, but she weighed only 3.25 lbs. This was small, as many at that time weighed 6.5 lbs.

The Maltese during the 19th century was in great demand; it

ON BRITISH SHORES

It is indeed possible that the Maltese arrived in Britain with the invading Romans, but some claim that it first made its appearance on British shores during the reign of King Henry VIII.

was considered a useful dog for hawkers to sell in the streets. The stains on neglected face hair were considered an advantage, for they suggested that the dog had been weeping and this obviously attracted some kind-hearted purchasers. The dog-seller would stand on the curbside, holding out a tiny Maltese in his hands, and would almost always attract a purchaser. One such seller even bandaged one of the dog's feet, which was said to have helped him considerably with his sales!

There was constant effort to produce smaller and smaller Maltese, but this was only to their detriment, for they generally grew to have low vitality and were difficult to breed. New blood was eventually introduced from the Continent, and this brought about certain changes. At first the dogs were rather large, but the breed resumed its desired weight of 4–9 lbs. and a generally hardier constitution was achieved.

Between the years of 1860 and 1870, the kennels of Mr. Mandeville in London were highly prominent, with his dogs winning well at all the major shows. As the century progressed, many of the Maltese went back to Mr. Mandeville's Maltese, Fido and Lilly.

J. H. Walsh, under the pen name "Stonehenge," wrote a wonderful book called *The Dog* in 1867. The few lines he wrote about the Maltese are worthy of quota-

GENUS *CANIS*

Dogs and wolves are members of the genus *Canis*. Wolves are known scientifically as *Canis lupus* while dogs are known as *Canis domesticus*. Dogs and wolves are known to interbreed. The term "canine" derives from the Latin-derived word *Canis*. The term "dog" has no scientific basis but has been used for thousands of years. The origin of the word "dog" has never been authoritatively ascertained.

tion: "This beautiful little dog is a Skye Terrier in miniature, with, however, a far more silky coat, a considerably shorter back, and a tail stiffly curved over the hip."

The breed became so scarce as to induce Sir Edwin Landseer to paint one as the last of the race.

Psyche, the Maltese bitch owned by Miss Gibbs, from an engraving circa 1867.

Drawing of an early Skye Terrier, bearing some resemblance to the Maltese, as it appeared in a drawing published in 1867.

After completion of the painting, several Maltese were imported from Malta, and, though still scarce, they were able to be obtained. The little bitch from which the portrait was sketched was the property of Miss Gibbs, or Morden, and was descended from parents imported by Mr. Lukey, direct from Manila.

The allusion to the Skye Terrier in the Stonehenge quotation may seem strange to observers of the breed today, but the Skye Terrier of that time did not look much like today's Skye. Several of the smaller long-coated breeds were likened to the Skye Terrier in the latter part of the 19th century, including the Lhasa Apso.

Hopping to the 20th century, like most breeds of dog in Britain, the Maltese was badly affected by World War I (1914–1918). Breeding was curtailed and the Maltese Club of London was sadly disbanded. It was believed at this time that there were no Maltese on the island of Malta, but when the war was over Miss Van Oppen (later Mrs. Roberts) eventually managed to buy four bitches on the Continent. She brought them to Britain, where they produced offspring in quarantine. Four additional imports came into Britain following this and, with the few dogs that had remained, the breed was again revived.

In the 1920s and early 1930s, there was an increasing, but still limited, number of registrations with The Kennel Club but sufficient interest was shown in the breed for the Maltese Club to be founded in 1934.

As the years progressed, the breed slowly moved its way up in popularity within the Toy Group, although the breed does not in

> **BRAIN AND BRAWN**
> Since dogs have been inbred for centuries, their physical and mental characteristics are constantly being changed to suit man's desires for hunting, retrieving, scenting, guarding and warming their masters' laps. During the past 150 years, dogs have been judged according to physical characteristics as well as functional abilities. Few breeds can boast a genuine balance between physique, working ability and temperament.

any way rank as numerically strong as the highly popular Cavalier King Charles Spaniel and Yorkshire Terrier. New registrations in Britain each year are generally now upwards of 500 but, given the numbers registered, there can be few dog lovers who have not seen, or at least heard of, this delightful and elegant breed. In the show ring, the Maltese has certainly made its mark, with the breed winning through to attain high honors at many championship events.

THE MALTESE IN THE US

Unfortunately, there are not really any well-kept records of early Maltese history in the US, so the only information that can reliably be accessed is from old show catalogs when initially the breed was included in the Miscellaneous Class. At the first Westminster Show, held in 1877, a white Maltese was entered, listed as a Maltese Lion Dog, and it is there-

fore logical that the breed existed in the US earlier than that date.

The American Kennel Club (AKC) accepted registration for the breed in 1888. One of those registered that year was Snips, a bitch whose pedigree was unknown but who we know was whelped in February 1886. The other, Topsey, was also a bitch and again her pedigree was unknown, but she appears to have been imported. The next Maltese to be registered in the US was whelped on March 4, 1900 and called Bebe. In this case, it is known that the sire was Toto and the dam was Contessa.

Clearly the breed had captured the interest of the American people in those early years, for before the turn of the century, the American Natural History Museum received three mounted specimens of the breed, two of these having been presented in 1896. These were important donations to the museum and through them the memory of early American dogs can be kept alive for posterity's sake.

Whelped in 1901, Mrs. C. S. Young's Ch. Thackeray Rob Roy was the first Maltese champion recorded by the AKC, and the first Best in Show winner is believed to have been Mrs. Carl Baumann's Ch. Sweetsir of Dyker, who won the award in 1912. That year there were about 27 Maltese registered with the AKC, so the breed was progressing well numerically, with people being attracted to the breed in increasing numbers.

During World War I, the Maltese suffered greatly in Britain but thankfully almost 200 were registered in America between 1914 and 1918. Several prefixes became prominent in the following years, one of which was Arr, owned by Agnes Rossman. This was a kennel that was to become well known for breeding small Maltese that were of high quality, something that made them highly sought after. The influential stud dog, Sir Toby of Arr, was bred by Agnes Rossman and owned by Eleanor Bancroft of the prominent Hale Farm kennel.

The breed built up steadily over the next few years, thanks to the solid foundation of the Arr and Hale Farm stock, but by the 1930s the breed was in decline. Only four dogs were bred in 1937 and four, all from the same litter, in 1939. All of these registrations were by Eleanor Bancroft.

Thankfully for the breed in America, a few dedicated owners saw to it that the Maltese survived, and particular mention should be made of Dr. and Mrs. Vincenzo Calvaresi, whose Villa Malta kennel was based on Hale Farm stock in the 1940s. They were indeed successful breeders, producing over 100 champions from their kennel. Ch. Toby of Villa Malta was owned by Mrs.

> ## "HENRY"—THE TOP TOY
> The top-winning Maltese at one time in the US was Ch. Sand Island Small Kraft Lite, known to all as "Henry." He was owned by Carol F. Andersen and professionally handled by Vicki Abbot. Henry was also the Top Toy Dog of all time in the US.

Virginia Leitch, whose Jon Vir breeding also played an important part in contributing to the survival of the breed. The Calvaresis exhibited some splendid teams of Maltese during the 1950s, and these attracted much publicity to the breed.

In the 1950s, Toni and Aennchen Antonelli and their Aennchen Maltese were highly prominent in the US, and one of the best known dogs bred by them was the bitch Ch. Aennchen Poona Dancer, who won 37 Best in Show awards and was owned by Larry Ward and Frank Oberstar.

As the years progressed, Virginia Leitch began to produce some quality small Maltese by using a retired stud dog from the Arr kennel. In this way, she also revived Arr bloodlines that might otherwise have been lost.

Later it was possible to introduce fresh blood from European countries, strengthening still further the quality of the kennels that had been built up in America. Ch. Joanchenn's Maya Dancer, owned by Mamie Gregory, won a record of 43 Best in Show awards, something that was not broken until the late 1990s by Ch. Sand Island Small Kraft Lite, who took 82 such awards. Owned by Carol Frances Anderson and handled by Vicki Abbot, this male was among America's Top Ten of all breeds and holds the high accolade of having won the Toy Group at Westminster in 1992.

The bitch, Ch. Ta-Jon's Tickle Me Silly toted up 103 Best in Show wins to become the top-winning Maltese of all time. Tammy Simon is her breeder/handler, and her owners are Marion and Samuel Lawrence.

In America, the Maltese is popular not only as a show dog but also as a pet, and ranks within the top 15 of all breeds, with more than 12,000 registered each year. Now they frequently win the Toy Group as well as Best in Show awards, and this is a breed that is always popular with the ringside audience. Indeed, today the Maltese in America is in good hands and breeders produce some fine specimens, well capable of achieving the very highest awards.

The Maltese (right) with a spitz dog. This illustration is dated 1881 and was printed in Vero Shaw's *Book of the Dog*.

MALTESE

The Maltese is a sweet-natured dog, alert and lively with a high level of intelligence. Although a small breed, categorized in the Toy Group, this is a soundly built little dog, capable of enjoying plenty of exercise and fun. It would be a mistake to consider the Maltese a "soft" little animal, for although not a terrier, the Maltese was considered as such for many years and his character is quite alert enough to display the occasional terrier trait. He was certainly capable of catching rats and is said to have caught the occasional badger. In Sir Richard Glynn's book *Champion Dogs of the World*, the Maltese is described as "an attractive little imp," which probably describes the breed in a nutshell! But if you want to know more, then read on.

Like the majority of smaller dogs, the Maltese is a reasonably long-lived breed, so this is another factor that must be seriously contemplated before deciding that this is really the breed for you. Clearly, when taking a new animal into your home, the ultimate aim will be that the dog remains with you for his entire life.

Despite various ups and downs through the course of history, the Maltese is now well established in many countries of the world. In the US alone, over 12,000 new puppies are registered with the American Kennel Club each year.

PERSONALITY

The Maltese has a certain "something" about him, demanding that people look at him, and to these looks he returns a kind of self-satisfied expression. He is certainly a vigorous little companion, full of humor and a sense of fun. Left to his own devices, he would willingly turn out mice and other small rodents from the barn, which is not always possible when a dog is kept in long coat. Certainly a Maltese will thoroughly enjoy the sights and smells of a country walk, although this can, it must be understood, badly damage a show coat.

Affectionate with his owners, the Maltese is quite an individualist and does not always take readily to strangers. This is a clean and fastidious breed, one that has understandably been a much-loved pet with a certain refine-

The Maltese is an intriguing dog that thrives on love and affection. Your puppy inherits his sweet nature from his parents.

ment about him. Having said that, a few have taken up the sport of mini-agility and others enjoy obedience work.

A fearless little dog despite his diminutive size, the Maltese can make a good watchdog for he is always alert and filled with determination. In the home, the Maltese is a perfect small house-dog, fitting in well with whatever the household routine.

MALTESE WITH CHILDREN

Provided that parents have trained their children to treat dogs gently, being neither rough nor aggressive, most Maltese enjoy playing with youngsters. It must, though, be understood that young children should always be supervised when in the company of dogs in order that accidents do not happen, however unintentional they might be. No matter how hardy your Maltese may be, he is still a fragile few pounds that can be badly injured by a boisterous child. The small size is attractive for children, who are also usually enchanted by the pretty appearance and long flowing coat. If yours is a show dog, do take care that a child doesn't decide to groom out (not-so-carefully) all the coat while you're not looking!

MALTESE WITH OTHER FAMILY PETS

Always when one animal is introduced to another, careful supervi-

Maltese and children usually get along well together. Children must be taught that the Maltese is a small, delicate animal, not a pretty toy, that must be handled with care.

sion is essential. Most Maltese are quite prepared to associate with other animals, but a lot understandably depends on the personality of the other. An older dog or cat may not take readily to a newcomer in the household, although others accept them well. When a Maltese does find another canine or feline friend, usually the relationship is lasting and sincere. Indeed, one of the dangers is mutual grooming between animal friends, which can play havoc with the long coat of the Maltese, especially behind the ears!

PHYSICAL CHARACTERISTICS

Small in size, the Maltese generally weighs about 4–6 lbs. and the height should not exceed 10 inches from ground to withers. This is a compact breed, with about the same length from withers to root of tail as the height at withers. Both males and females are pretty little dogs, although there is a distinction between the two.

COLOR AND COAT

The white coat is, of course, the breed's crowning glory, but regular attention is necessary to keep these flowing locks clean and in good condition. Most owners tie up the hair in a cute little topknot, showing the features of the face and helping to keep the hair away from the eyes. This adds to the overall attractive appearance of

TEAR STAINING
Face staining on the white Maltese is of genuine concern to many owners. Sometimes staining can be caused by blocked tear ducts or ingrown eyelashes, but most of the time it is primarily a cosmetic problem. There are now many products available to remedy tear staining.

the Maltese, certainly a breed that has many dedicated admirers, and deservedly so.

Although the long, white coat makes a splendid sight and needs regular attention, there is no undercoat, as in the case of the breed's cousin, the Bichon Frise. This makes the Maltese's coat a little easier to manage. An added advantage is that, provided it is

The topknot in several variations, initially used to keep the hair from the dog's eyes, has become an accepted way to enhance the Maltese's appearance.

kept in good condition, the coat will not shed all over your carpets and furniture.

The straight coat is silky in texture and should never be woolly, another important distinguishing feature between the Maltese and its close relations. Although of good length, it is important that the coat is not so long that it impedes action when the dog is moving. For the show dog, a coat can hide a multitude of sins, but a good judge will always feel carefully beneath the coat to check that a glamorously coated Maltese is also well constructed.

Coat color and coat presentation on the Maltese are very important, so owners of the breed must be prepared to put in a good deal of work to keep it in tip-top condition, never looking dirty or unkempt. A white coat will only stay clean if bathed frequently.

The color of the Maltese's coat is always white, but slight lemon markings are permissible. The whiteness of the coat contrasts strikingly against the black nose pigment and dark, oval eyes with their black haloes of dark skin surrounding them. Even the pads of the feet should be black.

HEALTH CONSIDERATIONS

In general, the Maltese is a healthy, hardy little dog, but as in so many other breeds, certain health problems can arise. However, if owners are aware of the problems that can occur, they are undoubtedly in a position to deal with them in the best manner possible. Some problems are genetic and are carried via heredity, but others are not.

SMALL AS A SQUIRREL
The Maltese has varied in size over the years, but in the past he was compared in size to a squirrel. It has been said many times that ladies used to carry them in their sleeves, and there are reports of them having carried dogs in their bosoms!

Obviously, in many cases, veterinary consultation and treatment are necessary, but many Maltese owners feel that this breed responds well to herbal and homeopathic remedies, so these are well worthy of consideration. An increasing number of vets now incorporate some homeopathy and other natural healing practices with their traditional methods of treating animal patients, though you may have a harder time finding such a vet.

LICKING

Sometimes even a minor irritation will cause a dog to lick at his own skin, and this can all too easily develop into a habit. In the Maltese, such licking is likely to make the white coat turn pink in color, so owners really do need to prevent this. Several good preparations are now available to dissuade a dog from licking; usually they taste rather bitter and the habit can frequently be stopped by use of such an agent.

LEG PROBLEMS

Many toy dogs and other small breeds suffer from trouble with the knee joints, known as luxating patella, though of course only a few individuals are thus affected. Responsible breeders have their breeding stock checked regularly by their vets in an endeavor to reduce the incidence. Another important factor is that a dog

OBESITY IN OLDER DOGS

Elderly Maltese can be prone to putting on excess weight. The profuse coat deceives an owner into thinking that the dog is of correct weight, when in fact he is too fat. Over-eating or feeding the wrong foods may be the cause. Often an older dog requires a slightly different diet than a younger one.

should not be overweight, as this is likely to make the problem worse. Many dogs with luxating patella live with this problem without experiencing pain, but surgery sometimes has to be undertaken and is often successful.

BLADDER STONES

Although found only infrequently, bladder stones can sometimes cause a problem, as they are found more often in small breeds than in larger ones. Symptoms include frequent passing of urine, blood in the urine, straining to pass water, general weakness, depression and loss of appetite.

Urgent veterinary attention is necessary, for stones in the bladder can lead to irreparable kidney damage and life can be lost as a result. In many cases, stones can be dissolved by special diet under veterinary supervision, but certain types require surgical removal.

TEETH
As with many of the other smaller breeds, some Maltese lose their teeth at a relatively early age. It is therefore important to pay close attention to the care of teeth and gums so that they remain as healthy as possible, thereby preventing decay, infection and resultant loss.

A big bundle of affection in a little package, the Maltese loves to be close to his owner.

Infection in the gums may not just stop there. The bacteria from this infection is carried through the bloodstream, the result of which can be disease of liver, kidney, heart and joints. This is all the more reason to realize that efficient dental care is of utmost importance throughout a dog's life. In addition to brushing and providing safe dental devices (nylon bones and the like), owners should bring their Maltese to their vets for dental checkups and thorough cleaning procedures.

BAD BREATH

Offensive breath is usually the result of problems with teeth and gums, but it can also be caused by indigestion or be related to the kidneys.

In cases of digestive problems giving rise to bad breath, charcoal, either in the form of tablets or granules, can often help. A useful aid to masking bad breath is the use of chlorophyll tablets.

EYE PROBLEMS

Because the Maltese is a coated breed, hair can cause irritation to the eyeball. This can result in conjunctivitis and is very likely to cause an excess of tear production. This, in consequence, causes tear staining below the eye, something often noticed on white and light-colored dogs. Clearly, attention is therefore

> **WEIGHING YOUR DOG**
> The easiest method of weighing your Maltese is on the bathroom scale. First weigh yourself alone, then a second time while holding the dog in your arms. Deduct the first weight from the second to obtain the accurate weight of your Maltese.

necessary to keep the eyes clean and this should be a routine aspect of grooming this breed.

Eye ulcers are also not unusual in small dogs and, at any sign of these, veterinary help should be sought quickly to prevent long-term damage. Often

A dog with healthy eyes and showing no tear stains.

becoming red, inflamed and sore. At this stage, the dog will scratch at the ear and may hold his head on one side because of the pain.

It is important that ears are kept clean at all times, but if infection does arise, a vet will usually be able to prescribe suitable drops for efficient treatment.

GRASS SEEDS
Because they are low to the ground and have long coats and long ears, Maltese occasionally pick up grass seeds, the barbed ends of which can penetrate right into the skin. Often they are picked up on the coat, but work their way down to the skin, where they cause pain and sometimes abscesses. They can even get

The Maltese's long hair can cause irritation to the eyes. For this reason, keeping the eye area clean and free of excess hair should be part of routine grooming from puppyhood.

they are caused by something as simple as a bump or maybe a scratch. Veterinary prescription of suitable eye ointment or eye drops usually clears up the problem quite quickly.

EAR PROBLEMS
Helped by the fact that the Maltese is such a light-colored dog, it should be easy to detect ear problems at the earliest opportunity. Signs of an infected ear include a brown, odorous discharge that leads to the ear

DO YOU WANT TO LIVE LONGER?
If you like to volunteer, it is wonderful if you can take your dog to a nursing home once a week for several hours. The elder community loves to have a dog with which to visit, and often your dog will bring a bit of companionship to someone who is lonely or somewhat detached from the world. You will be not only bringing happiness to someone else but also keeping your dog busy—and we haven't even mentioned the fact that it has been discovered that volunteering helps to increase your own longevity!

stuck inside the nostrils or between the pads of the feet. It is therefore always important to check the coat after a walk, particularly in late summer and autumn. At any sign of distress, the cause must be investigated immediately.

OTHER HEALTH PROBLEMS

It must be understood that there are many other health problems that can be suffered by dogs, but it is not possible to outline them all here. As you get to know your Maltese, you will also come to recognize if ever he is "off-color," at which time a quick trip to the vet can often help to "nip a problem in the bud" so that suitable care and any necessary medication may be given.

DOGS, DOGS, GOOD FOR YOUR HEART!

People usually purchase dogs for companionship, but studies show that dogs can help to improve their owners' health and level of activity, as well as lower a human's risk of coronary heart disease. Without even realizing it, when a person puts time into exercising, grooming and feeding a dog, he also puts more time into his own personal health care. Dog owners establish more routine schedules for their dogs to follow, which can have positive effects on their own health. Dogs also teach us patience, offer unconditional love and provide the joy of having a furry friend to pet!

Just like all dogs, Maltese love to play outdoors. However, their long coats make them susceptible to picking up seeds or other irritants. Check your Maltese's coat and skin regularly for any abnormalities.

MALTESE

The American Kennel Club (AKC) breed standard for the Maltese is effectively a "blueprint" for the breed. It sets down the various points of the dog in words, enabling a visual picture to be conjured up in the mind of the reader. However, this is more easily said than done. Not only do standards vary from country to country, but people's interpretations of breed standards vary also. It is this difference of interpretation that makes judges select different dogs for top honors, for their opinions differ as to which dog most closely fits the breed standard. That is not to say that a good dog does not win regularly under different judges, nor that an inferior dog may rarely even be placed at a show, at least not among quality competition.

As with most breeds, there are variances between the standard used in the US and that in Britain. I particularly like the opening paragraph of the AKC standard, describing the Maltese as a toy dog, "covered from head to foot with a mantle of long, silky, white hair." In America, he is described as being gentle-mannered and affectionate, while the British standard describes him as "sweet-tempered," both really saying the same thing.

Regarding color, in Britain the standard says that slight lemon markings are permissible, whereas the AKC standard is more specific, stating that "Light tan or lemon on the ears is permissible, but not desirable." Something quite different between the breed standards of the two countries is that in the US the teeth may either be an

The standards proposed by kennel clubs worldwide are designed to keep the Maltese consistent in type. Though the "perfect" breed specimen will never exist, the standard gives breeders a model to follow in their breeding programs.

even, "edge-to-edge" bite or a scissors bite. In Britain, only the latter is acceptable.

The controversial word "jaunty" is used in the AKC standard to describe movement, but it must be stressed that this is qualified by the description of a "smooth, flowing gait," going on to say that from the side "he gives an impression of rapid movement, size considered."

The breed standard given here is that authorized by the American Kennel Club; it has been in effect since March of 1964.

THE AMERICAN KENNEL CLUB STANDARD FOR THE MALTESE

General Appearance: The Maltese is a toy dog covered from head to foot with a mantle of long, silky, white hair. He is gentle-mannered and affectionate, eager and sprightly in action, and, despite his size, possessed of the vigor needed for the satisfactory companion.

Head: Of medium length and in proportion to the size of the dog. The skull is slightly rounded on top, the stop moderate. The drop ears are rather low set and heavily feathered with long hair that hangs close to the head. Eyes are set not too far apart; they are very dark and round, their black rims enhancing the gentle yet alert expression. The muzzle is

MEETING THE IDEAL
The American Kennel Club defines a standard as: "A description of the ideal dog of each recognized breed, to serve as an ideal against which dogs are judged at shows." This "blueprint" is drawn up by the breed's recognized parent club, approved by a majority of its membership, and then submitted to the AKC for approval. This is a complete departure from the way standards are handled in England, where all standards and changes are controlled by The Kennel Club.

The AKC states that "An understanding of any breed must begin with its standard. This applies to all dogs, not just those intended for showing." The picture that the standard draws of the dog's type, gait, temperament and structure is the guiding image used by breeders as they plan their programs.

of medium length, fine and tapered but not snipy. The nose is black. The teeth meet in an even, edge-to-edge bite, or in a scissors bite.

Neck: Sufficient length of neck is desirable as promoting a high carriage of the head.

Body: Compact, the height from the withers to the ground equaling the length from the withers to the root of the tail. Shoulder blades are sloping, the elbows well knit and held close to the body. The back is level in topline, the ribs well sprung. The chest is fairly deep, the loins taut, strong, and just slightly tucked up underneath.

Tail: A long-haired plume carried gracefully over the back, its tip lying to the side over the quarter.

Legs and Feet: Legs are fine-boned and nicely feathered. Forelegs are straight, their pastern joints well knit and devoid of appreciable bend. Hind legs are strong and moderately angulated at stifles and hocks. The feet are small and round, with toe pads black. Scraggly hairs on the feet may be trimmed to give a neater appearance.

Coat and Color: The coat is single, that is, without undercoat. It hangs long, flat, and silky over the sides of the body almost, if not quite, to the ground. The long head-hair may be tied up in a topknot or it may be left hanging. Any suggestion of kinkiness, curliness, or woolly texture is objectionable. Color, pure white. Light tan or lemon on the ears is permissible, but not desirable.

Size: Weight under 7 pounds, with from 4 to 6 pounds preferred. Overall quality is to be favored over size.

Gait: The Maltese moves with a jaunty, smooth, flowing gait.

Viewed from the side, he gives an impression of rapid movement, size considered. In the stride, the forelegs reach straight and free from the shoulders, with elbows close. Hind legs to move in a straight line. Cow-hocks or any suggestion of hind leg toeing in or out are faults.

Temperament: For all his diminutive size, the Maltese seems to be without fear. His trust and affectionate responsiveness are very appealing. He is among the gentlest mannered of all little dogs, yet he is lively and playful as well as vigorous.

Head study of correct type and structure, showing the unique topknot.

HEAD FAULTS

Eyes too large and light in color, nose pigment faded, foreface too long.

Eyes too small, set too close together; foreface too long and narrow;
topknot askew, disrupting balance; wavy coat.

A NOTE ON THE STANDARD

Although a great deal can be learned from the breed standard, only by seeing good-quality, typical specimens can you really learn to appreciate the breed's many merits. Close observation of the breed also enables one to recognize variations in type or faults when they occur. Therefore, readers interested in showing their Maltese should watch other dogs being exhibited, and learn as much as possible from established breeders and exhibitors.

It is sensible to attend judges' seminars, which are often hosted by breed clubs. These breed seminars feature expert judges who can explain the finer points of the breed, essentially opening a forum for discussion about the standard and the breed. There is usually a dog, or perhaps several, available for demonstration purposes, and there may even be an opportunity for participants to feel beneath the coat for the structure of the animal.

Just a few elaborations on the breed standard are, however, worthy of brief comment here. It is important that the eyes do not bulge and that they are dark brown in color, with black eye rims and dark haloes. The nose, too, must be black, as strong pigment is important on the white-coated Maltese. Once strength of pigment is lost in a breed, it is difficult to regain.

We know from the breed standard that movement should be "flowing," and if stifles are straight this cannot be so. In many cases (unless the shoulder is also upright) dogs that are too straight in stifle have a sloping topline, that is to say that the topline slopes upward towards the dog's hindquarters, this resulting in rather stilted, jerky movement, not at all typical of the breed.

The British breed standard merely asks for a "medium length" of neck, but the American standard states rather more explicitly that "Sufficient length of neck is desirable as promoting a high carriage of the head." Indeed carriage of head, influenced by length of neck and shoulder placement, is important in the Maltese. This breed is to have a proud carriage of head, giving that certain "something" that makes people look at him.

It should also be borne in mind that although the Maltese has a long coat, coats that are too long are all too easily trodden on, interfering with the free stride of the breed. The Maltese should be

FAULTS IN PROFILE

Short neck, steep shoulders, soft topline, long back.

Long back, lacking angulation at both ends, low tailset, high in rear.

BREEDER'S BLUEPRINT

If you are considering breeding your bitch, it is very important that you are familiar with the breed standard. Reputable breeders breed with the intention of producing dogs that are as close as possible to the standard and that contribute to the advancement of the breed. Study the standard for both physical appearance and temperament, and make certain your bitch and your chosen stud dog measure up.

a well-balanced little dog with a coat of correct length, but not overly long, so that the outline is altered. With the long-haired tail plume carried gracefully over the back, the picture is complete.

MALTESE

This type of "love-me" look has captured the hearts of many dog owners.

Compare the puppy to the well-groomed adult and you will see that the beauty of the full-grown Maltese is as appealing as the puppy cuteness.

You have probably decided on a Maltese as your pet of choice following a visit to the home of a friend or acquaintance, where you got to see an adorable Maltese looking clean and pretty, wandering happily around the house, joining politely in the family fun. Or perhaps he was lying in stately pose, his flowing, silky coat spread elegantly over the sofa. However, as a new owner, you must realize that a good deal of care, commitment and careful training goes into raising a bois-terous puppy so that your pet turns into a well-behaved adult.

In deciding to take on a new puppy, you will be committing yourself to many years of responsibility. No dog should be discarded after a few months, or even a few years, after the novelty has worn off. Instead, your Maltese should be joining your household to spend the rest of his days with you.

Although temperamentally a Maltese is much easier to look

after than many other breeds, you will still need to carry out a certain amount of training. Unlike some of the larger guarding breeds, the Maltese will not respond well to overly strict training. Instead you will need to take a firm but gentle approach in order to get the very best out of your pet.

A Maltese generally likes to be clean around the house, but you will need to teach your puppy what is and is not expected. You will need to be consistent in your instructions; it is no good accepting certain behavior one day and not the next. Not only will your puppy simply not understand, he will be utterly confused. Your Maltese will want to please you, so you will need to demonstrate clearly how your puppy is to achieve this.

Although the dog you are taking into your home will be small, and therefore probably less troublesome in many ways than a larger dog, there will undoubtedly be a period of settling in. This will be great fun, but you must be prepared for mishaps around the home during the first few weeks of your life together. It will be important that precious ornaments are kept well out of harm's way, and you will have to think twice about where you place hot cups of coffee or

BREEDING CONSIDERATIONS
The decision to breed your dog is one that must be considered carefully and researched thoroughly before moving into action. Some people believe that breeding will make their bitch happier or that it is an easy way to make money. Unfortunately, indiscriminate breeding only worsens the rampant problem of pet overpopulation, as well as putting a considerable dent in your pocketbook. As for the bitch, the entire process from mating through whelping is not an easy one and puts your pet under considerable stress. Last, but not least, consider whether or not you have the means to care for an entire litter of pups. Without a reputation in the field, your attempts to sell the pups may be unsuccessful.

ARE YOU PREPARED?

Unfortunately, when a puppy is bought by someone who does not take into consideration the time and attention that dog ownership requires, it is the puppy who suffers when he is either abandoned or placed in a shelter by a frustrated owner. So all of the "homework" you do in preparation for your pup's arrival will benefit you both. The more informed you are, the more you will know what to expect and the better equipped you will be to handle the ups and downs of raising a puppy. Hopefully, everyone in the household is willing to do his part in raising and caring for the pup. The anticipation of owning a dog often brings a lot of promises from excited family members: "I will walk him every day," "I will feed him," "I will house-train him," etc., but these things take time and effort, and promises can easily be forgotten once the novelty of the new pet has worn off.

anything breakable. Accidents can and do happen, so you will need to think ahead so as to avoid these.

Before making your commitment to a new puppy, do also think carefully about your future vacation plans. If you have thought things through carefully and discussed the matter thoroughly with all the members of your family, hopefully you will have come to the right decision. If you decide that a Maltese should join your family, this should be a happy, long-term relationship for all parties concerned.

BUYING A MALTESE PUPPY
Although you may be looking for a Maltese as a pet rather than a show dog, this does not mean that you want a dog that is in any way "second-rate." A caring breeder will have brought up the entire litter of puppies with the same amount of care and dedication, and a puppy destined for a pet home should be just as healthy as one that will appear in the show ring.

Because you have carefully selected this breed, you will want a Maltese that is a typical specimen, both in looks and in temperament. In your endeavors to find such a puppy, you will have to select the breeder with care. The American Kennel Club will almost certainly be able to give you names of contacts within Maltese breed clubs and all-breed clubs. These people can possibly put you in touch with breeders who may have puppies for sale. However, although they can point you in the right direction, it will be up to you to do your homework carefully.

Even though you are probably not looking for a show dog, it is always a good idea to visit a show so that you can see quality specimens of the breed. This will also give you an opportunity to meet breeders who will probably be able to answer some of your queries. In addition, you will get some idea about which breeders appear to take the best care of their stock, and which are likely to have given their puppies the best possible start in life.

When buying your puppy, you will need to know about vaccinations, those already given and those still due. It is important that any injections already given by a veterinarian can be supported by documentary evidence. A worming routine is also vital for any young puppy, so the breeder should be able to tell you exactly what treatment has been given, when it has been administered and how you should continue.

Clearly, when selecting a puppy, the one you choose must

"YOU BETTER SHOP AROUND!"

Finding a reputable breeder who sells healthy pups is very important, but make sure that the breeder you choose is not only someone you respect but also someone with whom you feel comfortable. Your breeder will be a resource long after you buy your puppy, and you must be able to call with reasonable questions without being made to feel like a pest! If you don't connect on a personal level, investigate some other breeders before making a final decision.

be in good condition. The coat should look clean and healthy and there should be no discharge from the eyes or nose. Ears should also be clean, and there should be absolutely no

TEMPERAMENT COUNTS

Your selection of a good puppy can be determined by your needs. A show potential or a good pet? It is your choice. Every puppy, however, should be of good temperament. Although show-quality puppies are bred and raised with emphasis on physical conformation, responsible breeders strive for equally good temperament. Do not buy from a breeder who concentrates solely on physical beauty at the expense of personality.

sign of parasites. Check that there is no rash on the skin, and, of course, the puppy you choose should not have any evidence of diarrhea.

As in several other breeds, a few Maltese puppies have umbilical hernias, which can be seen as a small lump on the tummy where the umbilical cord was attached. Clearly it is preferable not to have such a hernia on any puppy, but you should check for this at the outset and, if there is one, you should discuss the seriousness of this with the breeder. Most umbilical hernias are safe, but your vet should keep an eye on this in case an operation is needed.

Finally, a few words of advice. Always buy your puppy from a reputable breeder. You should never buy through a third party, something that happens all too often and may not even be realized by the purchaser. Always insist that you see the puppy's dam and, if possible, the sire. However, frequently the sire will not be owned by the breeder of the litter, but a photograph may be available for you to see—ideally, a photograph showing the sire winning at a dog show! Ask if the breeder has any other of the puppy's relations that you could meet. For example, there may be an older half-sister or -brother

and it would be interesting for you to see how they have turned out, their eventual size, coat quality, temperament and so on.

Be sure, too, that if you decide to buy a puppy, all relevant documentation is provided at the time of sale. You will need a copy of the pedigree, AKC registration certificate, vaccination certificates and a feeding chart so that you know exactly how the puppy has

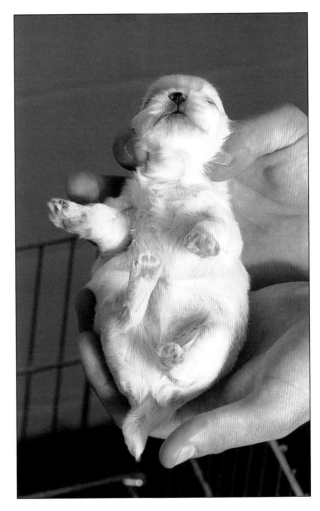

PUPPY APPEARANCE

Your puppy should have a well-fed appearance but not a distended abdomen, which may indicate worms or incorrect feeding, or both. The body should be firm, with a solid feel. The skin of the abdomen should be pale pink and clean, without signs of scratching or rash. Check the hind legs to make certain that dewclaws were removed, if any were present at birth.

been fed and how you should continue. Some careful breeders provide their puppy buyers with a small amount of food. This prevents the risk of an upset tummy, allowing for a gradual change of diet if that particular brand of food is not locally available.

At such a precious age, the Maltese pup is not ready for visitors. Breeders rarely allow visitors until the pups are at least four weeks old.

COMMITMENT OF OWNERSHIP

After considering all of these factors, you have most likely already made some very important decisions about selecting your Maltese puppy. If you have selected a breeder, you have gone a step further—you have done your research and found a responsible, conscientious person who breeds quality Maltese and who should be a reliable source of help as you and your puppy adjust to your new life together.

Even if you have not yet found the Maltese puppy of your dreams, observing litters will help you learn to recognize certain behavior and to determine what a pup's behavior indicates about his temperament. You will be able to pick out which pups are the leaders, which ones are less outgoing, which ones are confident, which ones are shy, playful, friendly, etc. Equally as important, you will learn to recognize what a healthy pup should look and act like. All of these things will help you in your search, and when you find the Maltese that was meant for you, you will know it!

Researching your breed, selecting a responsible breeder and observing as many pups as possible are all important steps on the way to dog ownership. It may seem like a lot of effort... and you have not even brought the pup home yet! Buying a puppy is not—or should not be—just another whimsical purchase. This is one instance in which you actually do get to choose your own family! You may be thinking that buying a puppy should be exciting—it should not be so serious and so

PEDIGREE VS. REGISTRATION CERTIFICATE

Too often new owners are confused between these two important documents. Your puppy's pedigree, essentially a family tree, is a written record of a dog's genealogy of three generations or more. The pedigree will show you the names as well as performance titles of all the dogs in your pup's background. Your breeder must provide you with a registration application, with his part properly filled out. You must complete the application and send it to the AKC with the proper fee. Every puppy must come from a litter that has been AKC-registered by the breeder, born in the US and from a sire and dam that are registered with the AKC.

The seller must provide you with complete records to identify the puppy. The AKC requires that the seller provide the buyer with the following: breed; sex, color and markings; date of birth; litter number (when available); names and registration numbers of the parents; breeder's name; and date sold or delivered.

PET INSURANCE
Just like you can insure your car, your house and your own health, you likewise can insure your dog's health. Investigate a pet insurance policy by talking to your vet. Depending on the age of your dog, the breed and the kind of coverage you desire, your policy can be very affordable. Most policies cover accidental injuries, poisoning and thousands of medical problems and illnesses, including cancers. Some carriers also offer routine care and immunization coverage.

much work. Keep in mind that your puppy is not a cuddly stuffed toy or table ornament, but a creature that will become a real member of your family. You will come to realize that, while buying a puppy is a pleasurable and exciting endeavor, it is not something to be taken lightly. Relax...the fun will start when the pup comes home!

Always keep in mind that a puppy is nothing more than a baby in a furry disguise...a baby who is virtually helpless in a human world and who trusts his

This is a lovely family portrait. If possible, observe at least one of the parents of your prospective pup to check for health and temperament. You can also see how the pups and parent(s) interact with each other.

owner for fulfillment of his basic needs for survival. In addition to food, water and shelter, your pup needs care, protection, guidance and love. If you are not prepared to commit to this, then you are not prepared to own a dog.

"Wait a minute," you say. "How hard could this be? All of my neighbors own dogs and they seem to be doing just fine. Why should I have to worry about all of this?" Well, you should not worry about it; in fact, you will probably find that once your Maltese pup gets used to his new home, he will fall into his place in the family quite naturally. But it never hurts to emphasize the commitment of dog ownership. With some time and patience, it is really not too difficult to raise a curious and exuberant Maltese pup to be a well-adjusted and well-mannered adult dog—a dog that could be your most loyal friend.

PREPARING PUPPY'S PLACE IN YOUR HOME

Researching your breed and finding a breeder are only two aspects of the "homework" you will have to do before bringing your Maltese puppy home. You will also have to prepare your home and family for the new addition. Much as you would prepare a nursery for a newborn baby, you will need to designate a place in your home that will be the puppy's own. How you prepare your home will depend on how much freedom the dog will be allowed. Whatever you decide, you must ensure that he has a place that he can "call his own."

When you bring your new puppy into your home, you are bringing him into what will become his home as well. Obviously, you did not buy a puppy so that he could take over your house, but in order for a puppy to grow into a stable, well-

ARE YOU A FIT OWNER?

If the breeder from whom you are buying a puppy asks you a lot of personal questions, do not be insulted. Such a breeder wants to be sure that you will be a fit provider for his puppy.

adjusted dog, he has to feel comfortable in his surroundings. Remember, he is leaving the warmth and security of his mother and littermates, as well as the familiarity of the only place he has ever known, so it is important to make his transition as easy as possible. By preparing a place in your home for the puppy, you are making him feel as welcome as possible in a strange new place. It should not take him long to get used to it, but the sudden shock of being transplanted is somewhat traumatic for a young pup. Imagine how a small child would feel in the same situation—that is how your puppy must be feeling. It is up to you to reassure him and to let him know, "Little baby, you are going to like it here!"

WHAT YOU SHOULD BUY

CRATE

To someone unfamiliar with the use of crates in dog training, it may seem like punishment to shut a dog in a crate, but this is not the case at all. Most breeders and trainers recommend crates as a preferred tool for pet puppies as well as show puppies. Crates are not cruel—crates have many humane and highly effective uses in dog care and training. For example, crate training is a very popular and very successful housebreaking

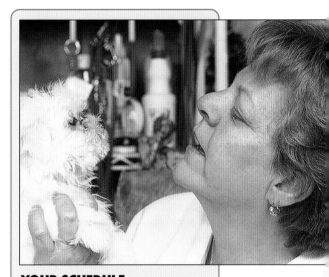

YOUR SCHEDULE . . .
If you lead an erratic, unpredictable life, with daily or weekly changes in your work requirements, consider the problems of owning a puppy. The new puppy has to be fed regularly, socialized (loved, petted, handled, introduced to other people) and, most importantly, allowed to go outdoors for house-training. As the dog gets older, he can be more tolerant of deviations in his feeding and relief schedule.

method. A crate can keep your dog safe during travel, and, perhaps most importantly, a crate provides your dog with a place of his own in your home. It serves as a "doggie bedroom" of sorts—your Maltese can curl up in his crate when he wants to sleep or when he just needs a break. Many dogs sleep in their crates overnight. When lined with soft bedding, a crate becomes a cozy pseudo-den for your dog. Like his ancestors, he too will seek out the comfort and retreat of a den—you just happen to be providing him with something a bit more luxu-

rious than what his early ancestors enjoyed.

As far as purchasing a crate, the type that you buy is up to you. It will most likely be one of the two most popular types: wire or fiberglass. There are advantages and disadvantages to each type. For example, a wire crate is more open, allowing the air to flow through and affording the dog a view of what is going on around him, while a fiberglass crate is sturdier and less drafty. Both can double as travel crates, providing protection for the dog. The smallest crate available at your pet shop will easily accommodate a Maltese puppy or adult.

QUALITY FOOD
All dogs need a good-quality food with an adequate supply of protein to develop their bones and muscles properly. Most dogs are not picky eaters but, unless fed properly, can quickly succumb to skin problems.

BEDDING
A soft crate pad in the dog's crate will help the dog feel more at home, and you may also like to give him a small blanket. This will take the place of the leaves, twigs, etc., that the pup

would use in the wild to make a den; the pup can make his own "burrow" in the crate. Although your pup is far removed from his den-making ancestors, the denning instinct is still a part of his genetic makeup. Second, until you bring your pup home, he has been sleeping amid the warmth of his mother and litter-mates, and while a blanket is not the same as a warm, breath-ing body, it still provides heat and something with which to snuggle. You will want to wash your pup's bedding frequently in case he has an accident in his crate, and replace or remove anything that becomes ragged and starts to fall apart.

Toys

Toys are a must for dogs of all ages, especially for curious playful pups. Puppies are the "children" of the dog world, and what child does not love toys? Chew toys provide enjoyment to both dog and owner—your dog will enjoy playing with his favorite toys, while you will

PHOTO COURTESY OF DOSKOCIL.

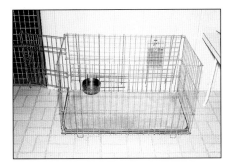

enjoy the fact that they distract him from your expensive shoes and leather sofa. Puppies love to chew; in fact, chewing is a physical need for pups as they are teething, and everything looks appetizing! The full range of your possessions—from throw pillows to Oriental carpet—are fair game in the eyes of a

Above: Your local pet shop should have a small crate to suit your Maltese.
Left: Wire crates are quite popular for use in the home.

This breeder utilizes portable wire enclosures to expose the litter to the activities of the home, while keeping them safely confined and out of danger.

teething pup. Puppies are not all that discerning when it comes to finding something to literally "sink their teeth into"—everything tastes great!

Maltese puppies can be active chewers and should be offered only the highest quality, safest toys. Breeders advise owners to resist stuffed toys, because they can become de-stuffed in no time. Similarly, squeaky toys are quite popular and can be used as an aid in training, but not for free play. If a pup "disembowels" one of these, the small plastic squeaker inside can be dangerous if swallowed. Monitor the condition of all your pup's toys carefully and get rid of any that have been chewed to the point of becoming potentially dangerous.

Be careful of natural bones, which have a tendency to splinter into sharp, dangerous pieces. Also be careful of rawhide, which can turn into pieces that are easy to swallow or into a mushy mess on your carpet.

LEASH

A nylon leash is probably the best option as it is the most resistant to puppy teeth should your pup take a liking to chewing on his leash. Of course, this is a habit that should be nipped in the bud, but if your pup likes to chew on his leash he has a very slim chance of being able

CRATE-TRAINING TIPS

During crate training, you should partition off the section of the crate in which the pup stays. If he is given too big an area, this will hinder your training efforts. Crate training is based on the fact that a dog does not like to soil his sleeping quarters, so it is ineffective to keep a pup in a crate that is so big that he can eliminate in one end and get far enough away from it to sleep. Also, you want to make the crate den-like for the pup. Blankets and a favorite toy will make the crate cozy for the small pup; as he grows, you may want to evict some of his "roommates" to make more room. It will take some coaxing at first, but be patient. Given some time to get used to it, your pup will adapt to his new home-within-a-home quite nicely.

to chew through the strong nylon. Nylon leashes are also lightweight, which is good for a young Maltese who is just getting used to the idea of walking on a leash. For everyday walking and safety purposes, the nylon leash is a good choice. As your pup grows up and gets used to walking on the leash, you may want to purchase a flexible leash. These leashes allow you to extend the length to give the dog a broader area to explore or to shorten the length to keep the dog close to you.

COLLAR
A lightweight nylon collar is a good choice; make sure that it fits snugly enough so that the

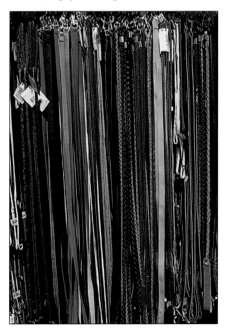

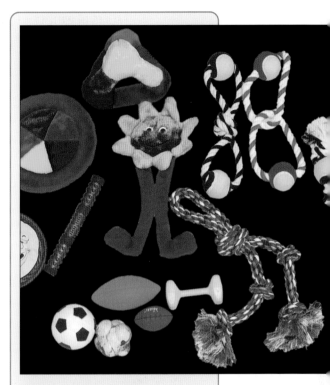

TOYS, TOYS, TOYS!
With a big variety of dog toys available, and so many that look like they would be a lot of fun for a dog, be careful in your selection. It is amazing what a set of puppy teeth can do to an innocent-looking toy; so, obviously, safety is a major consideration. Be sure to choose the most durable products that you can find. Hard nylon bones and toys are a safe bet, and many of them are offered in different scents and flavors that will be sure to capture your dog's attention. It is always fun to play a game of fetch with your dog, and there are balls and flying discs that are specially made to withstand dog teeth.

Your local pet shop will usually have a wide display of leashes. Select a very light leash for your Maltese.

CHOOSING THE RIGHT COLLAR

The **BUCKLE COLLAR** is the standard collar used for everyday purposes. Be sure that you adjust the buckle on growing puppies. Check it every day. It can become too tight overnight! These collars can be made of leather or nylon. Attach your dog's identification tags to this collar.

The **CHOKE COLLAR** is designed for training. It is constructed of highly polished steel so that it slides easily through the stainless steel loop. The idea is that the dog controls the pressure around his neck and he will stop pulling if the collar becomes uncomfortable. *Never* use a choke collar on a Maltese.

The **HALTER** is for a trained dog that has to be restrained to prevent running away, chasing a cat and the like. Considered the most humane of all collars, it is frequently used on smaller dogs for which collars are not comfortable.

pup cannot wriggle out of it, but is loose enough so that it will not be uncomfortably tight around the pup's neck. You should be able to fit a finger between the pup and the collar. It may take some time for your pup to get used to wearing the collar, but soon he will not even notice that it is there. Be certain that the collar is not damaging the Maltese's coat. Since your Maltese should spend most of his time indoors, you may wish to attach the collar only while he is outdoors.

FOOD AND WATER BOWLS

Your pup will need two bowls, one for food and one for water. Stainless steel or sturdy plastic bowls are popular choices. Many types can be purchased at a pet shop.

CLEANING SUPPLIES

Until a pup is house-trained, you will be doing a lot of cleaning. "Accidents" will occur, which is okay in the beginning because the puppy does not know any better. All you can do is be prepared to clean up any accidents. Old rags, paper towels, newspapers and a safe disinfectant are good to have on hand.

BEYOND THE BASICS

The items previously discussed are the bare necessities. You will find out what else you need as you go along—grooming supplies, flea/tick protection, baby gates to partition a room, etc. These things will vary depending on your situation, but it is important that you have everything you need to feed and make your Maltese comfortable in his first few days at home.

Breeders commonly introduce young puppies to crates or wire pens so that they are accustomed to the enclosures right away.

Your local pet shop sells an array of dishes and bowls for water and food.

PHOTO COURTESY OF MIKKI PET PRODUCTS.

PUPPY-PROOFING YOUR HOME

Aside from making sure that your Maltese will be comfortable in your home, you also have to make sure that your home is safe for your Maltese. This means taking precautions that your pup will not get into anything he should not get into and that there is nothing within his reach that may harm him should he sniff it, chew it, inspect it, etc. This probably seems obvious since, while you are primarily concerned with your pup's safety, at the same time you do not want your belongings to be ruined. Breakables should be placed out of reach if your dog is to have full run of the house. If he is to be limited to certain places within the house, keep any potentially dangerous items in the "off-limits" areas. An electrical cable can pose a danger should the puppy decide to taste it—cables should be fastened tightly against the wall. If your dog is going to spend time in a crate, make sure that there is nothing near his crate that he can reach if he sticks his curious little nose or paws through the openings. Just as you would with a child, keep all household cleaners and chemicals where the pup cannot get to them.

It is your responsibility to clean up after your dog has relieved himself. Pet shops have various aids to assist in the cleanup job.

DEWORMING

Ridding your puppy of worms is very important because they remove the nutrients that a growing puppy needs and certain worms that puppies carry, such as tapeworms and roundworms, can also infect humans.

Breeders initiate deworming programs at or about four weeks of age. The routine is repeated every two or three weeks until the puppy is three months old. The breeder from whom you obtained your puppy should provide you with the complete details of the deworming program.

Your veterinarian can prescribe and monitor the rest of the deworming program for you. The usual program is treating the puppy every 15–20 days until the puppy is positively worm-free. It is advised that you only treat your puppy with drugs that are recommended professionally.

It is also important to make sure that the outside of your home is safe. Of course, your puppy should never be unsupervised, but a pup let loose in the yard will want to run and explore, and he should be granted that freedom. Do not let a fence give you a false sense of security; you would be surprised how crafty (and persistent) a dog can be in figuring out how to dig under and squeeze his way through small holes. Be sure that the fence is well embedded into the ground and look out for any gaps in the fence that need repair. It doesn't

THE FIRST TWO WEEKS

It will take at least two weeks for your puppy to become accustomed to his new surroundings. Give him lots of love, attention, handling, frequent opportunities to relieve himself, a diet he likes to eat and a place he can call his own.

You will probably start feeding your pup the same food that he has been getting from the breeder; the breeder should give you a few days' supply to start you off. Although you should not give your pup too many treats, you will want to have puppy treats on hand for coaxing, training, rewards, etc. Be careful, though, as a small pup's calorie requirements are relatively low and a few treats can add up to almost a full day's worth of calories without the required nutrition.

require a large gap for the tiny Maltese to slip through. Remember that the breed has been compared to a squirrel! Fortunately, the Maltese cannot jump and climb like this little creature. Check the fence periodically to ensure that it is in good shape; a very determined pup may return to the same spot to "work on it" until he is able to get through.

FIRST TRIP TO THE VET

You have picked out your puppy, and your home and family are ready. Now all you have to do is collect your Maltese from the breeder and the fun begins, right? Well…not so fast. Something else you need to prepare is your pup's first trip to the veterinarian. Perhaps the breeder can recommend someone in the area who specializes in toy dogs or coated breeds, or maybe you know some other Maltese owners who can suggest a good vet. Either way, you should have an appointment arranged for your pup before you pick him up and plan on taking him for an examination before bringing him home.

The pup's first visit will consist of an overall examination to make sure that the pup does not have any problems that are not apparent to you. The veterinarian will also set up a schedule for the pup's vaccinations; the breeder will inform you of which ones the pup has already received and the vet can continue from there.

INTRODUCTION TO THE FAMILY

Everyone in the house will be excited about the puppy's coming home and will want to pet him and play with him, but it is best to make the introduction low-key so as not to overwhelm the puppy. He is apprehensive already. It is the first time he has been separated from his mother and the breeder, and the ride to your home is likely to be the first time he has been in a car. The last thing you want to do is smother him, as this will only frighten him further. This is not to say that human contact is not extremely necessary at this stage, because this is the time when a connection between the pup and his human family is formed. Gentle petting and soothing words should help console him, as well as just putting him down and letting him explore on his own (under your watchful eye, of course).

The pup may approach the family members or may busy himself with exploring for a while. Gradually, each person should spend some time with the pup, one at a time, crouching down to get as close to the pup's level as possible and

letting him sniff their hands and petting him gently. He definitely needs human attention and he needs to be touched—this is how to form an immediate bond. Just remember that the pup is experiencing a lot of things for the first time, at the same time. There are new people, new

HOW VACCINES WORK

If you've just bought a puppy, you surely know the importance of having your pup vaccinated, but do you understand how vaccines work? Vaccines contain the same bacteria or viruses that cause the disease you want to prevent, but they have been chemically modified so that they don't cause any harm. Instead, the vaccine causes your dog to produce antibodies that fight the harmful bacteria. Thus, if your dog is exposed to the disease in the future, the antibodies will destroy the viruses or bacteria.

noises, new smells and new things to investigate, so be gentle, be affectionate and be as comforting as you can be.

YOUR PUP'S FIRST NIGHT HOME

You have traveled home with your new charge safely in his crate or on a family member's lap. He's been to the vet for a thorough checkup; he's been weighed, his papers examined; perhaps he's even been vacci-

Seduction is one of the Maltese pup's many talents. Hold your ground when establishing the house rules.

nated and wormed as well. He's met the family, licked the whole family, including the excited children and the less-than-happy cat. He's explored his area, his new bed, the yard and anywhere else he's been permitted. He's eaten his first meal at home and relieved himself in the proper place. He's heard lots of new sounds, smelled new friends and seen more of the outside world than ever before.

That was just the first day! He's worn out and is ready for bed...or so you think!

It's puppy's first night and you are ready to say "Good night"—keep in mind that this is puppy's first night ever to be sleeping alone. His dam and littermates are no longer at paw's length and he's a bit scared, cold and lonely. Be reassuring to your new family member, but this is not the time to spoil him and give in to his inevitable whining.

Puppies whine. They whine to let the others know where

they are and hopefully to get company out of it. Place your pup in his new bed or crate in his room and close the crate door. Mercifully, he may fall asleep without a peep. When the inevitable occurs, ignore the whining; he is fine. Be strong and keep his interest in mind. Do not allow your heart to become guilty and visit the pup. He will fall asleep.

Many breeders recommend placing a piece of bedding from the breeder's home in his new bed so that he recognizes the scent of his littermates. Others still advise placing a hot water bottle in his bed for warmth. This latter may be a good idea provided the pup doesn't attempt to suckle—he'll get good and wet and may not fall asleep so fast.

Puppy's first night can be somewhat stressful for the pup and his new family. Remember that you are setting the tone of nighttime at your house. Unless you want to play with your pup every night at 10 p.m., midnight and 2 a.m., don't initiate the habit. Your family will thank you, and so will your pup!

PREVENTING PUPPY PROBLEMS

SOCIALIZATION
Now that you have done all of the preparatory work and have

PUPPY PROBLEMS
The majority of problems that are commonly seen in young pups will disappear as your dog gets older. However, how you deal with problems when he is young will determine how he reacts to discipline as an adult dog. It is important to establish who is boss (hopefully it will be you!) right away when you are first bonding with your dog. This bond will set the tone for the rest of your life together.

Socializing a
precious furry
creature like a
button-nosed
Maltese puppy is
one of every
owner's greatest
pleasures.

helped your pup get accustomed to his new home and family, it is about time for you to have some fun! Socializing your Maltese pup gives you the opportunity to show off your new friend, and your pup gets to reap the benefits of being an adorable furry creature that people will want to pet and, in general, think is absolutely precious!

Besides getting to know his new family, your puppy should be exposed to other people, animals and situations, but of course he must not come into close contact with dogs you don't know well until his course

PLAY'S THE THING

Teaching the puppy to play with his toys in running and fetching games is an ideal way to help the puppy develop muscle, learn motor skills and bond with you, his owner and master. He also needs to learn how to inhibit his bite reflex and never to use his teeth on people, forbidden objects and other animals in play. Whenever you play with your puppy, you make the rules. This becomes an important message to your puppy in teaching him that you are the pack leader and control everything he does in life. Once your dog accepts you as his leader, your relationship with him will be cemented for life.

The Maltese is an affectionate family dog who loves to be cuddled and pampered.

of injections is fully complete. Socialization will help him become well adjusted as he grows up and less prone to being timid or fearful of the new things he will encounter. Your pup's socialization began at the

> ### MANNERS MATTER
> During the socialization process, a puppy should meet people, experience different environments and definitely be exposed to other canines. Through playing and interacting with other dogs, your puppy will learn lessons, ranging from controlling the pressure of his jaws by biting his littermates to the inner-workings of the canine pack that he will apply to his human relationships for the rest of his life. That is why removing a puppy from his litter too early can be detrimental to the pup's development.

breeder's, but now it is your responsibility to continue it. The socialization he receives up until the age of 12 weeks is the most critical, as this is the time when he forms his impressions of the outside world. The eight-to-ten-week-old period, also known as the fear period, can be the Maltese's most delicate time period. If you have your Maltese at this young age, be sure that you are reassuring and gentle. Lack of socialization can manifest itself in fear and aggression as the dog grows up. He needs lots of human contact, affection, handling and exposure to other animals.

Once your pup has received his necessary vaccinations, feel free to take him out and about (on his leash, of course). Walk him around the neighborhood, take him on your daily errands, let people pet him, let him meet other dogs and pets, etc. Puppies do not have to try to make friends; there will be no shortage of people who will want to introduce themselves. Just make sure that you carefully supervise each meeting, especially with larger dogs that may be too aggressive for the gentle Maltese. If the neighborhood children want to say hello, for example, that is great—children and pups most often make great companions. Sometimes an excited child can unintentionally handle a pup too roughly, or an overzealous pup can playfully nip a little too hard. You want to make socialization experiences positive ones. What a pup learns during this very formative stage will affect his attitude toward future encounters. You want your dog to be comfortable around everyone. A pup that has a bad experience with a child may grow up to be a dog that is shy around or aggressive toward children.

CONSISTENCY IN TRAINING

Dogs, being pack animals, naturally need a leader, or else they try to establish dominance in their packs. When you bring a dog into your family, the choice of who becomes the leader and who becomes the "pack" is entirely up to you! Your pup's intuitive quest for dominance, coupled with the fact that it is nearly impossible to look at an adorable Maltese pup, with his dark "puppy-dog" eyes and angelic expression, and not cave in, give the pup almost an unfair advantage in getting the upper hand! A pup will definitely test the waters to see what he can and cannot do. Do not give in to those pleading eyes—stand your ground when it comes to disciplining the pup and make sure that all family members do the same. Avoid discrepancies by having all

DOG MEETS WORLD

Thorough socialization includes not only meeting new people but also being introduced to new experiences such as riding in the car, having his coat brushed, hearing the television, walking in a crowd—the list is endless. The more your Maltese experiences, and the more positive the experiences are, the less of a shock and the less frightening it will be for him to encounter new things.

members of the household decide on the rules before the pup even comes home...and be consistent in enforcing them! Early training shapes the dog's personality, so you cannot be unclear in what you expect.

COMMON PUPPY PROBLEMS

The best way to prevent puppy problems is to be proactive in stopping an undesirable behavior as soon as it starts. The old saying "You can't teach an old dog new tricks" does not necessarily hold true, but it is true that it is much easier to discourage bad behavior in a young developing pup than to wait until the

pup's bad behavior becomes the adult dog's bad habit. There are some problems that are especially prevalent in puppies as they develop.

NIPPING

As puppies start to teethe, they feel the need to sink their teeth into anything available...unfortunately that includes your fingers, arms, hair, and toes. You may find this behavior cute for the first five seconds...until you feel just how sharp those puppy teeth are. This is something you want to discourage immediately and consistently with a firm "No!" (or whatever number of firm "Nos" it takes for him to understand that you mean business). Then replace your finger with an appropriate chew toy. Your Maltese does not mean any harm with a friendly nip, but he also does not know how sharp his teeth can be.

CRYING/WHINING

Your pup will often cry, whine, whimper, howl or make some type of commotion when he is left alone. This is basically his way of calling out for attention to make sure that you know he is there and that you have not forgotten about him. He feels insecure when he is left alone, when you are out of the house and he is in his crate or when you are in another part of the

---

MENTAL AND DENTAL

Toys not only help your puppy get the physical and mental stimulation he needs but also provide a great way to keep his teeth clean. Hard rubber or nylon toys, especially those constructed with grooves, are designed to scrape away plaque, preventing bad breath and gum infection.

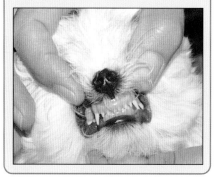

house and he cannot see you. The noise he is making is an expression of the anxiety he feels at being alone, so he needs to be taught that being alone is okay. You are not actually training the dog to stop making noise, you are training him to feel comfortable when he is alone and thus removing the need for him to make the noise. This is where the crate comes in handy. You want to know that he is safe when you are not there to supervise, and you know that he will be safe in his crate rather than roaming freely about the house. In order for the pup to stay in his crate without making a fuss, he needs to be comfortable in his crate. On that note, it is extremely important that the crate is never used as a form of punishment, or the pup will have a negative association with the crate.

Accustom the pup to the crate in short, gradually increasing time intervals in which you put him in the crate, maybe with a treat, and stay in the room with him. If he cries or makes a fuss, do not go to him, but stay in his sight. Gradually he will realize that staying in his crate is okay without your help, and it will not be so traumatic for him when you are not around. You may want to leave the radio on softly when you leave the house; the sound of human voices may be comforting to him.

CHEWING TIPS

Chewing goes hand in hand with nipping in the sense that a teething puppy is always looking for a way to soothe his aching gums. In this case, instead of chewing on you, he may have taken a liking to your favorite shoe or something else which he should not be chewing. Again, realize that this is a normal canine behavior that does not need to be discouraged, only redirected. Your pup just needs to be taught what is acceptable to chew on and what is off-limits. Consistently tell him "No!" when you catch him chewing on something forbidden and give him a chew toy.

Conversely, praise him when you catch him chewing on something appropriate. In this way, you are discouraging the inappropriate behavior and reinforcing the desired behavior. The puppy's chewing should stop after his adult teeth have come in, but an adult dog continues to chew for various reasons—perhaps because he is bored, needs to relieve tension or just likes to chew. That is why it is important to redirect his chewing when he is still young.

DIETARY AND FEEDING CONSIDERATIONS

Today the choices of food for your Maltese are many and varied. There are simply dozens of brands of food in all sorts of flavors and textures, ranging from puppy diets to those for seniors. There are even hypoallergenic and low-calorie diets available. Because your Maltese's food has a bearing on coat, health and temperament, it is essential that the most suitable diet be selected for a Maltese of his age. It is fair to say, however, that even dedicated owners can be somewhat perplexed by the enormous range of foods available. Only understanding what is best for your dog will help you reach a decision.

Dog foods are produced in three basic types: dry, semi-moist and canned. Dry foods are useful for the cost-conscious for overall they tend to be less expensive than semi-moist or canned. These contain the least fat and the most preservatives. In general, canned foods are made up of 60–70% water, while semi-moist ones often contain so much sugar that they are perhaps the least preferred by owners, even though their dogs seem to like them.

When selecting your dog's diet, three stages of development must be considered: the puppy stage, the adult stage and the senior stage.

STORING DOG FOOD

You must store your dry dog food carefully. Open packages of dog food quickly lose their vitamin value, usually within 90 days of being opened. Mold spores and vermin could also contaminate the food.

PUPPY STAGE

Puppies instinctively want to suck milk from their mother's teats and a normal puppy will exhibit this behavior from just a few moments following birth. If puppies do not attempt to suckle within the first half-hour or so, the breeder must encourage them to do so by placing them on a nipple, having selected ones with plenty of milk. This early milk supply is important in providing colostrum to protect the puppies during the first eight to ten weeks of their lives. Although a mother's milk is much better than any milk formula, despite there being some excellent ones available, if the puppies do not feed, they have to be hand-fed. Puppies should be allowed to nurse from their mothers for about the first six weeks, although from the third or fourth week the breeder will begin to introduce small portions of suitable solid food. Most breeders like to introduce alternate milk and meat meals initially, building up to weaning time.

By the time the puppies are seven or a maximum of eight weeks old, they should be fully weaned and fed solely on a proprietary puppy food. Selection of the most suitable, good-quality diet at this time is essential for a puppy's fastest growth rate is during the first year of

in certain circumstances additional vitamins, minerals and proteins will not be required.

ADULT DIETS

A dog is considered an adult when it has stopped growing, so in general the diet of a Maltese can be changed to an adult one at about 12 months of age, sometimes sooner depending on your selection of diet. There are many specially prepared diets available, but do keep in mind that

The Maltese can be introduced to adult kibble at around one year of age. Small-bite kibble is best for the Maltese.

life. Veterinarians are usually able to offer advice in this regard. The frequency of meals will be reduced over time, and when a young Maltese has reached the age of about 12 months, he can be switched onto an adult-maintenance diet.

Puppy and junior diets should be well balanced for the needs of your dog, so that except

---

FEEDING TIPS

- Dog food must be served at room temperature, neither too hot nor too cold. Fresh water, changed daily and served in a clean bowl, is mandatory, especially when feeding dry food.
- Never feed your dog from the table while you are eating, and never feed your dog leftovers from your own meal. They usually contain too much fat and too much seasoning.
- Dogs must chew their food. Hard pellets are excellent; soups and stews are to be avoided.
- Don't add leftovers or any extras to commercial dog food. The normal food is usually balanced, and adding something extra destroys the balance.
- Except for age-related changes, dogs do not require dietary variations. They can be fed the same diet, day after day, without becoming bored or ill.

A Worthy Investment

Veterinary studies have proven that a balanced high-quality diet pays off in your dog's coat quality, behavior and activity level. Invest in premium brands for the maximum payoff with your dog.

adult Maltese generally do not require a high protein content. This applies particularly to those that have been spayed or neutered. Something else to consider is that too much milk, or other dairy products, can sometimes cause an upset tummy.

SENIOR DIETS

As dogs get older, their metabolism changes. The older dog usually exercises less, moves more slowly and sleeps more. This change in lifestyle and physiological performance requires a change in diet. Since these changes take place slowly, they might not be recognizable. What is more readily recognizable is weight gain. By continuing to feed your dog an adult-maintenance diet when he is slowing down metabolically, your dog will gain weight.

Adults and pups have different dietary needs. Discuss your feeding plans with your breeder and veterinarian.

> ### "DOES THIS COLLAR MAKE ME LOOK FAT?"
> While humans may obsess about how they look and how trim their bodies are, many people believe that extra weight on their dogs is a good thing. The truth is, pets should not be over- or under-weight, as both can lead to or signal sickness. In order to tell how fit your pet is, run your hands over his ribs. Are his ribs buried under a layer of fat or are they sticking out considerably? If your pet is within his normal weight range, you should be able to feel the ribs easily, but they should not protrude abnormally. If you stand above him, the outline of his body should resemble an hourglass. Some breeds do tend to be leaner while some are a bit stockier, but making sure your dog is the right weight for his breed will certainly contribute to his good health.

Obesity in an older dog compounds the health problems that already accompany old age.

As your dog gets older, few of his organs function up to par. The kidneys slow down and the intestines become less efficient. These age-related factors are best handled with a change in diet and a change in feeding schedule to give smaller portions that are more easily digested.

There is no single best diet for every older dog. While many dogs do well on light or senior diets, other dogs do better on or other special premium diets such as lamb and rice. Be sensitive to your senior Maltese's diet and this will help control other problems that may arise with your old friend.

WATER

Just as your dog needs proper nutrition from his food, water is an essential "nutrient" as well. Water keeps the dog's body properly hydrated and promotes normal function of the body's systems. During housebreaking, it is necessary to keep an eye on how much water your Maltese is drinking, but once he is reliably trained he should have access to clean fresh water at all times. Make certain that the dog's water bowl is clean, and change the water often, making sure that water is always available for your dog, especially if you feed dry food.

EXERCISE

Although Maltese are small, all dogs require some form of exercise, regardless of breed. A sedentary lifestyle is as harmful to a dog as it is to a person. The Maltese is not an overly active breed. Regular walks, play sessions in the yard or letting the dog run free in the fenced yard under your supervision are sufficient forms of exercise for the Maltese.

DRINK, DRANK, DRUNK— MAKE IT A DOUBLE

In both humans and dogs, as well as other living organisms, water forms the major part of nearly every body tissue. Naturally, we take water for granted, but without it, life as we know it would cease.

For dogs, water is needed to keep their bodies functioning biochemically. Additionally, water is needed to replace the water lost while panting. Unlike humans, who are able to sweat to dissipate heat, dogs must pant to cool down, thereby losing the vital water from their bodies need to regulate their body temperatures. Humans lose electrolyte-containing products and other body-fluid components through sweating; dogs do not lose anything except water.

Water is essential always, but especially so when the weather is hot or humid or when your dog is exercising or working vigorously.

CHANGE IN DIET

As your dog's caretaker, you know the importance of keeping his diet consistent, but sometimes when you run out of food or if you're on vacation, you have to make a change quickly. Some dogs will experience digestive problems, but most will not. If you are planning on changing your dog's menu, do so gradually to ensure that your dog will not have any problems. Over a period of four to five days, slowly add some new food to your dog's old food, increasing the percentage of new food each day.

Bear in mind that an overweight dog should never be suddenly over-exercised; instead he should be allowed to increase exercise slowly. Not only is exercise essential to keep the dog's body fit, it also is essential to his mental well-being. A bored dog will find something to do, which often manifests itself in some type of destructive behavior. In this sense, it is essential for the owner's mental well-being as well!

GROOMING

Your Maltese will need to be groomed regularly, so it is essential that short grooming sessions be introduced from a very early age. From the very beginning, a few minutes each day should be set aside, the duration building up slowly as the puppy matures and the coat grows in length.

Different breeders use varying methods of grooming and you will undoubtedly find the particular way that suits you best. Some owners even groom their dogs on their laps, but most do so on a grooming table. It is important that the table has a non-slip surface, and under no circumstances leave your Maltese alone on the table, for he may all too easily jump off and injure himself.

EARLY TRAINING

When the puppy is used to standing on the table, you will probably find it useful to teach him to be rolled over onto his back. This you will do by putting your hand on the puppy's back, your fingers pointing toward the head. The other hand will be used underneath, cupping the rib cage. Turn the puppy over gently and hold him there reassuringly, speaking to him all the while and stroking him. Do not at this early stage attempt to do anything that would hurt the puppy, for he will need to regard this as a pleasurable experience. To begin with, you must always be sure to have one hand firmly in control in case the puppy wriggles. In the event of his wriggling and turning back again, just repeat the exercise, always remembering that it is you who must have the upper hand. Be firm, but always kind and gentle.

When you know he is comfortable with this, introduce a few gentle brush strokes with your pin brush and then with a wide-toothed comb. This may take a little getting used to both for you and your puppy, but if your Maltese learns to lie over, you will more easily be able to groom in all the awkward places, paying special attention to the "armpits," the groin area and under the chin. You both will be glad you had a little patience to learn this trick from the very start!

It is worth mentioning that some people prefer their dogs to lie over on their sides instead. This can be taught by supporting the front legs and part of the side

WALKING LIKE A PRO

For many people, it is difficult to imagine putting their dog's well-being in someone else's hands, but if you are unable to give your dog his necessary exercise breaks, hiring a professional dog walker may be a good idea. Dog walkers offer your dog exercise, a chance to work off energy and companionship—all things that keep your dog healthy. Seek referrals from your veterinarian, breeder or groomer to find a reputable dog walker.

Never groom a coat when it is completely dry. On the occasions when you are grooming without bathing, use a fine water spray or light coat conditioner that will help to avoid removing too much coat. This will also prevent hair breakage.

Doubtless you will pick up some grooming tips from other Maltese enthusiasts if you visit shows, and in time you will undoubtedly decide upon the method that best suits you and your dog.

Either grooming on a table or, if you prefer, on your lap, work

with one hand, the back legs and hips with the other, and gently rolling the dog over on the table, allowing your own body to move over with him to make him feel at ease. Again you will need to hold him securely and reassure him gently until he is comfortable with the procedure.

ROUTINE GROOMING

To keep your Maltese looking in tip-top condition, it is important to keep the coat clean and to groom regularly, even between baths. All grooming equipment must be kept clean so that it does not snag the hair, and combs with teeth missing should never be used for they can so easily damage a coat, and worse!

GROOMING EQUIPMENT
- Pure bristle brush
- Good-quality pin brush
- Wide-toothed comb (metal or stainless steel)
- Fine-toothed comb
- Scissors
- Dental elastics and elastic bands
- Bows
- Blow dryer
- Dog shampoo
- Dog conditioner
- Shower or shower attachment
- Rubber mat
- Towels
- Nail clippers
- Liquid ear cleaner
- Tissues/cotton balls
- Tooth-cleaning aid
- Paper or plastic for wrapping (if required)

methodically through the coat, using a pure bristle brush for most of the work. Many people like to commence at the tail end and work forward, but always make sure that you work right down to the skin. If you groom only the top coat, you will find that knots form near to the skin and these can be difficult and painful to remove. If you do come across knots, which can happen, especially if debris from a walk has not been noticed immediately upon your return home, work these out with your fingers first of all. Work always from the inside outward, for if you tackle the knot the other way around it will only get tighter. Also take care never to catch the comb in the narrow bones of the tail.

When each section of the coat is groomed through, you should finish it off, either with your pin brush or comb. Finally, with the dog standing on a table, put a nice straight parting along the back, working from the neck end backwards.

THE HEAD

It is necessary for your Maltese to have been trained to stay still while the head furnishings are dealt with, especially when putting in the topknot. But before the topknot goes in, the head furnishings must be thoroughly groomed out, brushing the head

hair up, away from the eyes, and then working down the ears and cheeks.

It is important that the eyes are kept meticulously clean, so use a moistened cotton ball to

TIPPING THE SCALES

Good nutrition is vital to your dog's health, but many people end up overfeeding or giving unnecessary supplements. Here are some common doggie diet don'ts:

- Adding milk, yogurt and cheese to your dog's diet may seem like a good idea for coat and skin care, but dairy products are very fattening and can cause indigestion.
- Diets high in fat will not cause heart attacks in dogs but will certainly cause your dog to gain weight.
- Most importantly, don't assume your dog will simply stop eating once he doesn't need any more food. Given the chance, he will eat you out of house and home!

The Maltese's puppy coat is easier to care for than the full adult coat, but still needs regular attention. Start by brushing the pup gently with a pin brush.

Different ways of doing up the head furnishings of the Maltese vary from place to place, either a single topknot in the center or setting the hair in two topknots.

To create a single topknot, when the hair has been brushed away from the eyes, the tip of the comb should be used to draw a line from the outer corner of each eye, finishing just before the edge of the ears, with a line drawn across the skull. The hair is then attached by a small dental elastic, but never too tightly. For a double topknot, you will need to make a central parting from between the eyes, subsequently forming a topknot on each side of the head. Most people like to finish off the topknot with a neat little bow. These can be purchased especially for this purpose. It is important to remember that when replacing the topknot, the dental elastic must be cut out carefully, never pulled, or this would break the coat. Also, care must be taken not to cut any coat out in the process!

remove any significant debris from the corners of the eyes. Then comb through very carefully, using a fine-toothed comb. Try not to remove any hair in the process, for if you do so it will take time to grow in again and meanwhile will not lie evenly with the rest of the coat. Tear staining is common in all white-coated dogs, so attention to cleanliness around the eyes is particularly important.

BATHING AND DRYING

How frequently you decide to bathe your Maltese will depend very much on whether yours is a show dog or a pet. Show dogs are usually washed before every show, which may be as frequently as once a week. Pet dogs are usually washed less often. It is, however, essential that the coat is fully groomed through prior to washing, for a coat with tangles emerges from the bath with even tighter ones!

As with grooming, every owner has his own preference as to how best to wash. I like to stand my own dogs on a non-slip mat in the bathtub (some Maltese owners prefer to use a suitable sink), then wet the coat thoroughly using a shower attachment to rinse. It is imperative that the water temperature be previously tested on your own hand. Use a good-quality shampoo designed especially for dogs,

Special techniques are used by professional groomers. If possible, watch a professional work on your Maltese to help you learn how to groom him yourself.

The head and facial furnishings are very important to the Maltese's overall expression. Tying up the topknot is a skill that takes practice.

Your Maltese requires considerable grooming with special combs and brushes. Your breeder or a groomer can advise you of what you need to groom your dog at home.

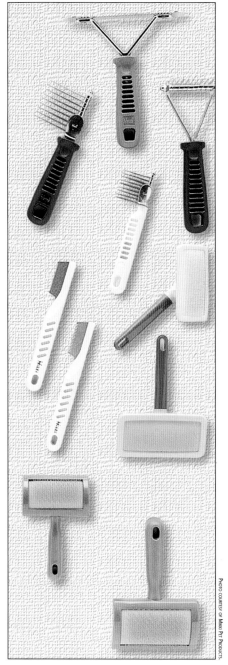

indeed some are now especially suitable for the white coat of a Maltese. Always stroke the shampoo into the coat rather than rub, so as not to create knots. When this has been thoroughly rinsed out, apply a canine coat conditioner in the same manner and follow the manufacturer's instructions regarding length of time it should be left in the coat. Then rinse again until the water runs clear. Many people like to use a baby shampoo on the head to avoid irritation to the eyes, and some like to plug the ears with cotton balls to avoid water getting inside them. Personally, I use neither of these, but by taking care especially in that area, I have never encountered problems. Finally, lift your dog carefully out of the bath, wrapped in a warm, clean towel. Undoubtedly your dog will want to shake—so be prepared!

Drying can be done on whichever table you use for the grooming process or even on your lap. Work systematically, applying warm air from the blow dryer, and concentrating on one area at a time. For best effect, the coat that is not being dried should be kept in a damp towel. When you have completed one side of the dog, the towel on which the dog is lying should be replaced by a dry one while you work on the opposite side. Use

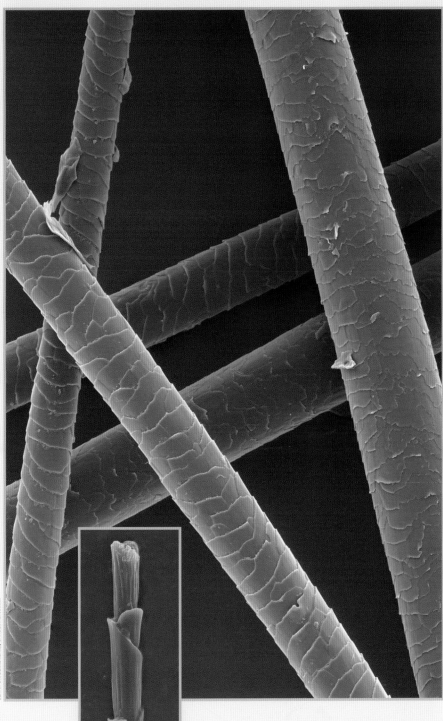

Normal hairs of a dog enlarged 200 times original size. The cuticle (outer covering) is clean and healthy. Unlike human hair that grows from the base, a dog's hair also grows from the end, as shown in the inset.

The Maltese's coat should be thoroughly wet before commencing the bathing process.

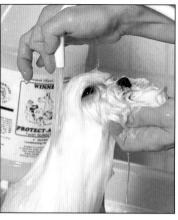

A cup with warm water and dog shampoo can be used to distribute the shampoo evenly over the dog's body.

Massage the shampoo gently into the dog's coat, being careful not to create knots and being especially cautious around the face. The face requires gentle handling to keep soap from the dog's eyes.

BATHING BEAUTY

Once you are sure that the dog is thoroughly rinsed, squeeze the excess water out of his coat with your hand and dry him with an heavy towel. You may choose to use a blow dryer on his coat or just let it dry naturally. In cold weather, never allow your dog outside with a wet coat.

There are "dry bath" products on the market, which are sprays and powders intended for spot cleaning, that can be used between regular baths if necessary. They are not substitutes for regular baths, but they are easy to use for touch-ups as they do not require rinsing.

the blow dryer to blow air downwards from the skin toward the tips of the hairs, brushing through gently as you dry.

The head is usually left until last and is best handled with the dog in a sitting position. Many dogs do not like warm air blowing directly towards their eyes and nose, so do take this into consideration when angling the blow dryer.

TRIMMING

Trimming below the pads of the feet prevents uncomfortable hairballs from forming between the pads. On males, most owners also trim a little hair from the end of the penis, but a good half inch must be left so that tiny hairs do not aggravate the penis and set up infection. Also, take care not to cut through a female's nipple, and remember that males have little nipples too!

After drying with a towel, much of the excess water should be removed from the dog's coat.

Various types of blow dryers are available for drying your Maltese. Use warm, not hot, air, as the Maltese's skin is sensitive.

This Maltese gets another thorough brushing after his coat has been dried.

SOAP IT UP

The use of human soap products like shampoo, bubble bath and hand soap can be damaging to a dog's coat and skin. Human products are too strong; they remove the protective oils coating the dog's hair and skin that make him water-resistant. Use only shampoo made especially for dogs. You may like to use a medicated shampoo, which will help to keep external parasites at bay.

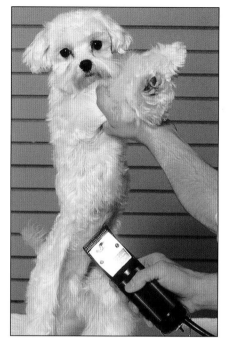

Pet Maltese often are not kept in full coat. The groomer uses electric clippers on the dog's body to give him a pet trim.

The face requires special attention. Here, a fine-toothed comb is used on a puppy's facial furnishings.

The facial hair on an adult in full coat requires even more attention.

CRACKERING

Crackering the coat is also known as wrapping. Some breeders and exhibitors of Maltese do this as an aid to coat growth, but it is certainly not used by everyone, and is rarely done by pet owners.

Crackering is something of an art that cannot be learned overnight, and incorrect wrapping can damage rather than enhance a coat. It is important that new Maltese owners who wish to cracker their dogs' coats gain practical experience from a dedicated enthusiast.

This procedure involves oiling the coat and then, taking small strips of hair, wrapping each section either in paper or in plastic, secured by an elastic band. Each packet then needs to be opened and the coat brushed through thoroughly every one or two days, so it is a time-consuming procedure. This is by no means a replacement for grooming, but an added task for those who choose to undertake it.

EAR CLEANING

On a Maltese, hair will also grow inside the ears. This should be carefully plucked out with blunt-ended tweezers. Remove only a few hairs at a time and this should be entirely painless. Ears must always be kept clean. This can be done using a special liquid cleaner with cotton balls, but extreme care must be taken not to delve too deeply into the ears as this can cause injury. Be on the lookout for any signs of infection or ear-mite infestation. If your Maltese has been shaking his head or scratching at his ears frequently, this usually indicates a problem. If his ears have an unusual odor, this is a sure sign of mite infestation or infection, and a signal to have his ears checked by the veterinarian.

Nail Clipping

Your Maltese should be accustomed to having his nails trimmed at an early age, since it will be part of your maintenance routine throughout his life. Long nails are uncomfortable for any dog and can be sharp enough to scratch someone unintentionally. Also, a long nail has a better chance of ripping and bleeding, or causing the foot to spread. A good rule of thumb is that if you can hear your dog's nails' clicking on the floor when he walks, his nails are too long.

Before you start cutting, make sure you can identify the "quick" in each nail. The quick is a blood vessel that runs through the center of each nail and grows rather close to the end. It will bleed if accidentally cut, which will be quite painful for the dog as it contains nerve endings. Keep some type of clotting agent on hand, such as a styptic pencil

Whether puppy coat, pet trim or full coat, a final once-over with a fine-toothed comb will finish the grooming nicely.

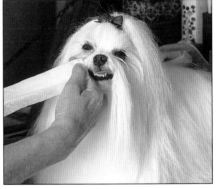

"Crackering" or "wrapping" is usually only done on show dogs to protect the coat and aid in its growth.

The groomer uses elastic bands to section off the dog's hair while trimming.

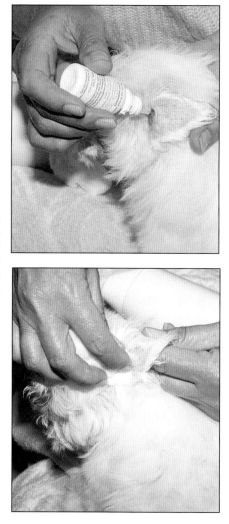

Ear cleaning is important. Special drops or powder assist in the ear cleaning process, along with cotton balls.

next nail. It is better to clip a little at a time, particularly with black-nailed dogs.

Hold your pup steady as you begin trimming his nails; you do not want him to make any sudden movements or run away. Talk to him soothingly and stroke him as you clip. Holding his foot in your hand, simply take off the end of each nail in one quick clip. You can purchase nail clippers that are specially made for dogs; you can probably find them wherever you buy pet supplies.

TRAVELING WITH YOUR MALTESE

CAR TRAVEL

You should accustom your Maltese to riding in a car at an early age. You may or may not take him in the car often, but at the very least he will need to go to the vet and you do not want these trips to be traumatic for the dog or for you. The safest way for a dog to ride in the car is in his crate. If he uses a crate in the house, you can use the same crate for travel. Put the pup in the crate and see how he reacts. If the puppy seems uneasy, you can have a passenger hold him on his lap while you drive. Do not let the dog roam loose in the vehicle—this is very dangerous! If you should stop short, your dog can be thrown and injured. If the dog starts climbing on you

or styptic powder (the type used for shaving). This will stop the bleeding quickly when applied to the end of the cut nail. Do not panic if you cut the quick, just stop the bleeding and talk soothingly to your dog. Once he has calmed down, move on to the

PEDICURE TIP

A dog that spends a lot of time outside on a hard surface, such as cement or pavement, will have his nails naturally worn down and may not need to have them trimmed as often, except maybe in the colder months when he is not outside as much. Regardless, it is best to get your dog accustomed to the nail-trimming procedure at an early age so that he is used to it. Some dogs are especially sensitive about having their feet touched, but if a dog has experienced it since puppyhood, it should not bother him.

Until your Maltese is accustomed to having his nails clipped, you may need to have someone else hold the pup while you do the clipping.

Pet shops sell nail clippers made especially for dogs.

and pestering you while you are driving, you will not be able to concentrate on the road. It is an unsafe situation for everyone—human and canine.

For long trips, be prepared to stop to let the dog relieve himself. Bring along whatever

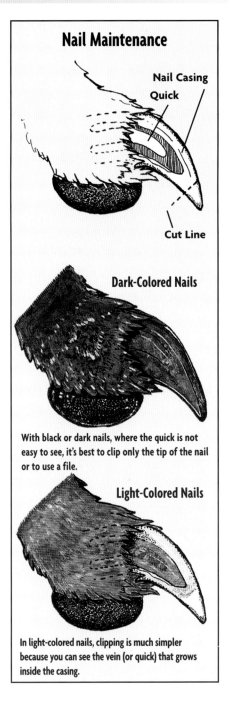

Nail Maintenance

Nail Casing
Quick
Cut Line

Dark-Colored Nails

With black or dark nails, where the quick is not easy to see, it's best to clip only the tip of the nail or to use a file.

Light-Colored Nails

In light-colored nails, clipping is much simpler because you can see the vein (or quick) that grows inside the casing.

you need to clean up after him. You should take along some paper towels and perhaps some rags for use should he have a potty accident in the car or suffer from motion sickness.

FLYING WITH YOUR MALTESE
Contact your chosen airline before proceeding with your travel plans that include your Maltese. The dog will be required to travel in a fiberglass crate and you should always check in advance with the airline regarding specific requirements for the crate's size, type and labeling. To help put the dog

ABUSING YOUR BEST FRIEND

As an educated and caring pet owner, you may believe that everyone wants to invest countless hours (and dollars) in order to raise a loving and well-adjusted canine companion. Sadly, this is not the case, as dogs account for almost half of all victims of animal abuse. Remember, abuse implies not only beating or torturing an animal but also neglecting the animal, such as failing to provide adequate shelter and food or emotional fulfillment.

at ease, give him one of his favorite toys in the crate. Do not feed the dog for several hours prior to checking in so that you minimize his need to relieve himself. However, some airlines require that the dog must be fed within a certain time frame of arriving at the airport. In any case, a light meal is best.

Make sure your dog is properly identified and that your contact information appears on his ID tags and on his crate. Although most dogs travel in a different area of the plane than the human passengers, the Maltese is fortunate enough to travel in "coach" (or "first-class") along with his owners! Most airlines provide for Toy dogs to travel with their owners, and Maltese owners should always seek out airlines willing to accommodate their dogs first!

BOARDING

So you want to take a family vacation—and you want to include *all* members of the family. You would probably make arrangements for accommodations ahead of time anyway, but this is especially important when traveling with a dog. You do not want to make an overnight stop at the only place around for miles and find out that they do not allow dogs. Also, you do not want to reserve a place for your family without

MOTION SICKNESS
*If life is a motorway...*your dog may not want to come along for the ride! Some dogs experience motion sickness in cars that leads to excessive salivation and even vomiting. In most cases, your dog will fare better in the familiar, safe confines of his crate. To desensitize your dog, try going on several short jaunts before trying a long trip. If your dog experiences distress when riding in the vehicle, drive with him only when absolutely necessary, and do not feed him or give him water before you go.

confirming that you are travelling with a dog because, if it is against their policy, you may not have a place to stay.

Alternatively, if you are traveling and choose not to bring your Maltese, you will have to make arrangements for him while you are away. Some options are to take him to a neighbor's house to stay while you are gone, to have a trusted neighbor stop by often or stay at your house or to bring your dog to a reputable boarding kennel. If you choose to board him at a kennel, you should visit in advance to see the facilities provided, how clean they are and where the dogs are kept. Talk to some of the employees and see how they treat the dogs. Learn if they have experience in grooming long-coated dogs, if they spend time with the dogs, play with them, exercise them, etc.? Also find out the kennel's policy on vaccinations and what they require. This is for all of the dogs' safety, since when dogs are kept together, there is a greater risk of diseases being passed from dog to dog. You may even be able to board your Maltese at your veterinarian's office. Explore this option, too.

ON THE ROAD

If you are going on a long car trip with your dog, be sure the hotels are dog-friendly. Many hotels do not accept dogs. Also take along some ice that can be thawed and offered to your dog if he becomes overheated. Most dogs like to lick ice.

IDENTIFICATION

Your Maltese is your valued companion and friend. That is why you always keep a close eye

The selection of a boarding kennel is important. If you need to board your Maltese, be certain that the kennel you choose has experience with small dogs and will give your dog personal attention.

on him and you have made sure that he cannot escape from the yard or wriggle out of his collar and run away from you. However, accidents can happen and there may come a time when your dog unexpectedly gets separated from you. If this unfortunate event should occur, the first thing on your mind will be finding him. Proper identification, including an ID tag, and possibly a tattoo and/or a microchip, will increase the chances of his being returned to you safely and quickly.

IDENTITY CRISIS!

Surely you know the importance of good nutrition, good training and a good home, but are you aware of the importance of identification tags for your dog? If your dog ran away or got lost, ID tags on your pet's collar would provide crucial information such as the dog's name, and your name and address, making it possible that your dog would soon be returned. Every morning before taking your dog out, make sure his collar and tags are present and securely fastened.

This Maltese is tattooed on her belly. Tattooing is a permanent form of identification. Tattooed dogs have a better chance of being returned to their owners if they become lost or stolen.

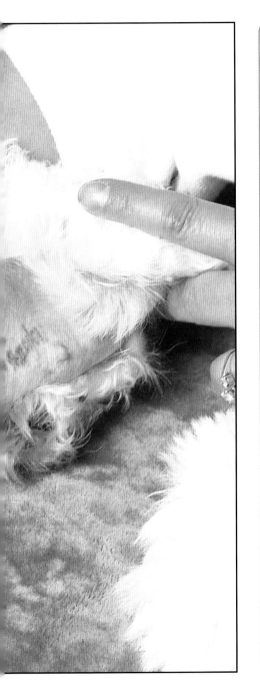

IDENTIFICATION OPTIONS

As puppies become more and more expensive, especially those puppies of high quality for showing and/or breeding, they have a greater chance of being stolen. The usual collar dog tag is, of course, easily removed. But there are two more permanent techniques that have become widely used for identification of dogs.

The puppy microchip implantation involves the injection of a small microchip, about the size of a corn kernel, under the skin of the dog. If your dog shows up at a clinic or shelter, or is offered for resale under less-than-savory circumstances, he can be positively identified by the microchip. The microchip is scanned, and a registry quickly identifies you as the owner.

Tattooing is done on various parts of the dog, from his belly to his ears. The number tattooed can be your telephone number or any other number that you can easily memorize. When professional dog thieves see a tattooed dog, they usually lose interest. For the safety of our dogs, no laboratory facility or dog broker will accept a tattooed dog as stock.

Discuss microchipping and tattooing with your veterinarian and breeder. Some vets perform these services on their own premises for a reasonable fee. To ensure that your dog's ID will be effective, be certain that the dog is then properly registered with a legitimate national database.

Training your Maltese is all about communicating with the dog in a way he understands and keeping his attention throughout the lesson.

Living with an untrained dog is a lot like owning a piano that you do not know how to play—it is a nice object to look at, but it does not do much more than that to bring you pleasure. Now try taking piano lessons, and suddenly the piano comes alive and brings forth magical sounds and rhythms that set your heart singing and your body swaying.

The same is true with your Maltese. Any dog is a big responsibility and if not trained

sensibly may develop unacceptable behavior that annoys you or could even cause your family friction.

To train your Maltese, you may like to enroll in an obedience class. Teach him good manners as you learn how and why he behaves the way he does. Find out how to communicate with your dog and how to recognize and understand his communications with you. Suddenly the dog takes on a new role in your life—he is clever, interesting, well behaved and fun to be with. He demonstrates his bond of devotion to you daily. In other words, your Maltese does wonders for your

OBEDIENCE SCHOOL

Taking your dog to an obedience school may be the best investment in time and money you can ever make. You will enjoy the benefits for the lifetime of your dog and you will have the opportunity to meet people who have similar expectations for their companion dogs.

ego because he constantly reminds you that you are not only his leader, you are his hero!

Those involved with teaching dog obedience and counseling owners about their dogs' behavior have discovered some interesting facts about dog ownership. For example, train-

Whether your Maltese is destined to be a world-class show dog or simply a world-class pet dog, training is an absolute necessity.

FREE AT LAST!

While running off-leash may be great fun for your dog, it can turn into a time when your dog shows you everything you did wrong in obedience class. If you want to give your dog a chance to have some fun and exercise without the constraints of a leash, the best place to do this is in a designated fenced-in area where dogs can socialize and work off excess energy. When visiting such an area, don't let your dog run amok or unattended, watch other dogs that are present and follow all rules, specifically those regarding waste disposal.

ing dogs when they are puppies results in the highest rate of success in developing well-mannered and well-adjusted adult dogs. Training an older dog, from six months to six years of age, can produce almost equal results, providing that the owner accepts the dog's slower rate of learning capability and is willing to work patiently to help the dog succeed at developing to his fullest potential. Unfortunately, many owners of untrained adult dogs lack the patience factor, so they do not persist until their dogs are successful at learning particular behaviors.

Training a puppy, aged 10 to 16 weeks (20 weeks at the most), is like working with a dry sponge in a pool of water. The pup soaks up whatever you show him and constantly looks for more things to do and learn. At this early age, his body is not yet producing hormones, and therein lies the reason for such a high rate of success. Without hormones, he is focused on his owners and not particularly interested in investigating other places, dogs, people, etc. You are his leader: his provider of food, water, shelter and security. He latches onto you and wants to stay close. He will usually follow you from room to room, will not let you out of his sight when you are outdoors with him and will respond in like manner to the people and animals you encounter. If you greet a friend warmly, he will be happy to greet the person as well. If, however, you are hesitant or anxious about the approach of a stranger, he will respond accordingly.

Once the puppy begins to produce hormones, his natural curiosity emerges and he begins to investigate the world around him. It is at this time when you may notice that the untrained dog begins to wander away from you and even ignore your commands to stay close.

Often there are classes within a reasonable distance of the owner's home, but you can also do a lot to train your dog yourself. Sometimes there are classes available but the tuition is too costly. Whatever the circumstances, the solution to training your Maltese without formal obedience lessons lies within the pages of this book.

CALM DOWN
Dogs will do anything for your attention. If you reward the dog when he is calm and attentive, you will develop a well-mannered dog. If, on the other hand, you greet your dog excitedly and encourage him to wrestle with you, the dog will greet you the same way and you will have a hyperactive dog on your hands.

This chapter is devoted to helping you train your Maltese at home. If the recommended procedures are followed faithfully, you may expect positive results that will prove rewarding to both you and your dog.

Whether your new charge is a puppy or a mature adult, the methods of teaching and the techniques we use in training basic behaviors are the same. After all, no dog, whether puppy

A big part of housebreaking your Maltese is having a securely fenced yard in which he can relieve himself. This metal fence is too short to confine even a tiny Maltese.

Setting limits is a big part of training. A curious Maltese will not hesitate to snoop around, so you must decide where the dog is and is not allowed to go in the home.

mind from the outset that when your puppy is old enough to go out in public places, any canine deposits must be removed at once. You will always have to carry with you a small plastic bag or "poop-scoop."

Outdoor training includes such surfaces as grass, dirt and cement. Indoor training usually means training your dog to newspaper. When deciding on the surface and location that you will want your Maltese to use, be sure it is going to be permanent. Training your dog to grass and then changing your mind two months later is extremely difficult for both dog and owner.

Next, choose the command you will use each and every time you want your puppy to void. "Be quick," "Hurry up" and "Potty" are examples of commands commonly used by dog owners. Get in the habit of giving the puppy your chosen relief command before you take

or adult, likes harsh or inhumane methods. All creatures, however, respond favorably to gentle motivational methods and sincere praise and encouragement.

HOUSEBREAKING

You can train a puppy to relieve himself wherever you choose, but this must be somewhere suitable. You should bear in

MEALTIME

Mealtime should be a peaceful time for your puppy. Do not put his food and water bowls in a high-traffic area in the house. For example, give him his own little corner of the kitchen where he can eat undisturbed and where he will not be underfoot. Do not allow small children or other family members to disturb the pup when he is eating.

him out. That way, when he becomes an adult, you will be able to determine if he wants to go out when you ask him. A confirmation will be signs of interest, such as wagging his tail, watching you intently, going to the door, etc.

PUPPY'S NEEDS

The puppy needs to relieve himself after play periods, after each meal, after he has been sleeping and any time he indicates that he is looking for a place to urinate or defecate. The urinary and intestinal tract muscles of very young puppies are not fully developed. Therefore, like human babies, puppies need to relieve themselves frequently.

Take your puppy out often—every hour for an eight-week-old, for example, and always immediately after sleeping and eating. The older the puppy, the less often he will need to relieve himself. Finally, as a mature healthy adult, he will require only three to five relief trips per day.

HOUSING

Since the types of housing and control you provide for your puppy have a direct relationship on the success of house-training, we consider the various aspects of both before we begin training. Bringing a new puppy home and turning him loose in your house can be compared to turning a child loose in a sports arena and telling the child that the place is all his! The sheer enormity of the place would be too much for him to handle.

Instead, offer the puppy clearly defined areas where he can play, sleep, eat and live. A room of the house where the family gathers is the most obvious choice. Puppies are social animals and need to feel a part

PLAN TO PLAY

The puppy should also have regular play and exercise sessions when he is with you or a family member. Exercise for a very young puppy can consist of a short walk around the house or yard. Playing can include fetching games with a large ball or a special toy. (All puppies teethe and need soft things upon which to chew.) Remember to restrict play periods to indoors within his living area (the family room, for example) until he is completely house-trained.

of the pack right from the start. Hearing your voice, watching you while you are doing things and smelling you nearby are all positive reinforcers that he is now a member of your pack. Usually a family room, the kitchen or a nearby adjoining dining area is ideal for provid-

When getting your Maltese to pay attention, you do not want to over-excite him.

PAPER CAPER

Never line your pup's sleeping area with newspaper. Puppy litters are usually raised on newspaper and, once in your home, the puppy will immediately associate newspaper with voiding. Never put newspaper on any floor while house-training, as this will only confuse the puppy. If you are paper-training him, use paper in his designated relief area only. Finally, restrict water intake after evening meals. Offer a few licks at a time—never let a young puppy gulp water after meals.

---

ing safety and security for both puppy and owner.

Within that room there should be a smaller area which the puppy can call his own. An alcove, a wire or fiberglass dog crate or a fenced (not boarded!) corner from which he can view the activities of his new family will be fine. The size of the area or crate is the key factor here. The area must be large enough for the puppy to lie down and stretch out, yet small enough so that he cannot relieve himself at one end and sleep at the other without coming into contact with his droppings until fully trained to relieve himself outside. The designated area should be lined with clean bedding and a toy. Water must always be available in a non-spill container.

CANINE DEVELOPMENT SCHEDULE

It is important to understand how and at what age a puppy develops into adulthood. If you are a puppy owner, consult the following Canine Development Schedule to determine the stage of development your puppy is currently experiencing. This knowledge will help you as you work with the puppy in the weeks and months ahead.

Period	Age	Characteristics
FIRST TO THIRD	BIRTH TO SEVEN WEEKS	Puppy needs food, sleep and warmth, and responds to simple and gentle touching. Needs mother for security and disciplining. Needs littermates for learning and interacting with other dogs. Pup learns to function within a pack and learns pack order of dominance. Begin socializing with adults and children for short periods. Begins to become aware of his environment.
FOURTH	EIGHT TO TWELVE WEEKS	Brain is fully developed. Needs socializing with outside world. Remove from mother and littermates. Needs to change from canine pack to human pack. Human dominance necessary. Fear period occurs between 8 and 16 weeks. Avoid fright and pain.
FIFTH	THIRTEEN TO SIXTEEN WEEKS	Training and formal obedience should begin. Less association with other dogs, more with people, places, situations. Period will pass easily if you remember this is pup's change-to-adolescence time. Be firm and fair. Flight instinct prominent. Permissiveness and over-disciplining can do permanent damage. Praise for good behavior.
JUVENILE	FOUR TO EIGHT MONTHS	Another fear period about 7 to 8 months of age. It passes quickly, but be cautious of fright and pain. Sexual maturity reached. Dominant traits established. Dog should understand sit, down, come and stay by now.

NOTE: THESE ARE APPROXIMATE TIME FRAMES. ALLOW FOR INDIVIDUAL DIFFERENCES IN PUPPIES.

PARENTAL GUIDANCE

Training a dog is a life experience. Many parents admit that much of what they know about raising children they learned from caring for their dogs. Dogs respond to love, fairness and guidance, just as children do. Become a good dog owner and you may become an even better parent.

Dogs are, by nature, clean animals and will not remain close to their relief areas unless forced to do so. In those cases, they then become dirty dogs and usually remain that way for life.

CONTROL

By *control*, we mean helping the puppy to create a lifestyle pattern that will be compatible to that of his human pack (*you*!). Just as we guide little children to learn our way of life, we must show the puppy when it is time to play, eat, sleep, exercise and even entertain himself.

Your puppy should always sleep in his crate. He should also learn that, during times of household confusion and excessive human activity such as at breakfast when family members are preparing for the day, he can play by himself in relative safety and comfort in his designated area. Each time you leave the puppy alone, he should understand exactly where he is to stay. You can gradually increase the time he is left alone to get him used to it. Puppies are chewers. They cannot tell the difference between things like lamp cords, television wires, shoes, table legs, etc. Chewing into a television wire, for example, can be fatal to the puppy while a shorted wire can start a fire in the house.

If the puppy chews on the arm of the chair when he is alone, you will probably discipline him angrily when you get home. Thus, he makes the association that your coming home means he is going to be punished. (He will not remember chewing the chair and is incapable of making the association of the discipline with his naughty deed.)

Other times of excitement, such as visits, family parties, etc., can be fun for the puppy, providing he can view the activities from the security of his designated area. He is not underfoot and he is not being fed all sorts of tidbits that will probably cause him stomach distress, yet he still feels a part of the fun.

SCHEDULE

A puppy should be taken to his relief area each time he is released from his designated area, after meals, after play sessions, when he first awakens in the morning (at age eight weeks, this can mean 5 a.m.!). The puppy will indicate that he's ready "to go" by circling or sniffing busily—do not misinterpret these signs. For a puppy less than ten weeks of age, a routine of taking him out every hour is necessary. As the puppy grows, he will be able to wait for longer periods of time.

Safe travel is but one of the many benefits of accustoming your Maltese to a crate. These dogs are being taken to a dog show, each in his own crate.

Keep trips to his relief area short. Stay no more than five or six minutes and then return to the house. If he goes during that time, praise him lavishly and take him indoors immediately. If he does not, but he has an accident when you go back indoors,

---

TAKE THE LEAD

Do not carry your dog to his relief area. Lead him there on a leash or, better yet, encourage him to follow you to the spot. If you start carrying him to his spot, you might end up doing this routine forever and your dog will have the satisfaction of having trained *you.*

pick him up immediately, say "No! No!" and return to his relief area. Wait a few minutes, then return to the house again. Never hit a puppy or put his face in urine or excrement when he has an accident!

Once indoors, put the puppy in his crate until you have had time to clean up his mess. Then release him to the family area and watch him more closely than before. Chances are, his accident was a result of your not picking up his signal or waiting too long before offering him the opportunity to relieve himself. Never hold a grudge against the puppy for accidents.

Let the puppy learn that going outdoors means it is time to relieve himself, not play. Once trained, he will be able to play indoors and out and still differentiate between the times for play versus the times for relief. Help him develop regular hours for naps, being alone, playing by himself and just resting, all in his crate. Encourage him to entertain himself while you are busy with your activities. Let him learn that having you near is comforting, but it is not your main purpose in life to provide him with undivided attention.

Each time you put your puppy in his own area, use the same command, whatever suits best. Soon, he will run to his crate or special area when he hears you say those words. Crate training provides safety for you, the puppy and the home. It also provides the puppy with a feel-

THE CLEAN LIFE

By providing sleeping and resting quarters that fit the dog, and offering frequent opportunities to relieve himself outside his quarters, the puppy quickly learns that the outdoors (or the newspaper if you are training him to paper) is the place to go when he needs to urinate or defecate. It also reinforces his innate desire to keep his sleeping quarters clean. This, in turn, helps develop the muscle control that will eventually produce a dog with clean living habits.

ing of security, and that helps the puppy achieve self-confidence and clean habits.

Remember that one of the primary ingredients in house-training your puppy is control. Regardless of your lifestyle, there will always be occasions when you will need to have a place where your dog can stay and be happy and safe. Crate training is the answer for now and in the future.

In conclusion, a few key elements are really all you need for a successful house-training method—consistency, frequency, praise, control and supervision. By following these procedures with a normal, healthy puppy, you and the puppy will soon be past the stage of accidents and ready to move on to a full and rewarding life together.

ROLES OF DISCIPLINE, REWARD AND PUNISHMENT

Discipline, training one to act in accordance with rules, brings

A crate mat and a soft blanket make this Maltese's crate a cozy den from which he can safely observe the goings-on of the house.

THE GOLDEN RULE

The golden rule of dog training is simple. For each "question" (command), there is only one correct answer (reaction). One command = one reaction. Keep practicing the command until the dog reacts correctly without hesitating. Be repetitive but not monotonous. Dogs get bored just as people do!

order to life. It is as simple as that. Without discipline, particularly in a group society, chaos reigns supreme and the group will eventually perish. Humans and canines are social animals and need some form of discipline in order to function effectively. They must procure food, protect their home base and reproduce to keep the species going. If there were no discipline in the lives of social animals, they would eventually die from starvation and/or predation by other stronger animals. In the case of domestic canines, dogs need discipline in their lives in order to understand how their pack (you and other family members) functions and how they must act in order to survive.

A large humane society in a highly populated area recently surveyed dog owners regarding their satisfaction with their relationships with their dogs. People who had trained their

THE SUCCESS METHOD

Success that comes by luck is usually short-lived. Success that comes by well-thought-out proven methods is often more easily achieved and permanent. This is the Success Method. It is designed to give you, the puppy owner, a simple yet proven way to help your puppy develop clean living habits and a feeling of security in his new environment.

6 Steps to Successful Crate Training

1 Tell the puppy "Crate time!" and place him in the crate with a small treat (a piece of cheese or half of a biscuit). Let him stay in the crate for five minutes while you are in the same room. Then release him and praise lavishly. Never release him when he is fussing. Wait until he is quiet before you let him out.

2 Repeat Step 1 several times a day.

3 The next day, place the puppy in the crate as before. Let him stay there for ten minutes. Do this several times.

4 Continue building time in five-minute increments until the puppy stays in his crate for 30 minutes with you in the room. Always take him to his relief area after prolonged periods in his crate.

5 Now go back to Step 1 and let the puppy stay in his crate for five minutes, this time while you are out of the room.

6 Once again, build crate time in five-minute increments with you out of the room. When the puppy will stay willingly in his crate (he may even fall asleep!) for 30 minutes with you out of the room, he will be ready to stay in it for several hours at a time.

dogs were 75% more satisfied with their pets than those who had never trained their dogs.

Dr. Edward Thorndike, a noted psychologist, established *Thorndike's Theory of Learning*, which states that a behavior that results in a pleasant event tends to be repeated. Likewise, a behavior that results in an unpleasant event tends not to be repeated. It is this theory on which training methods are based today. For example, if you manipulate a dog to perform a specific behavior and reward him for doing it, he is likely to do it again because he enjoyed the end result.

Occasionally, punishment, a penalty inflicted for an offense, is necessary. The best type of punishment often comes from an outside source. For example, a child is told not to touch the stove because he may get burned. He disobeys and touches the stove. In doing so, he receives a burn. From that time on, he respects the heat of the stove and avoids contact with it. Therefore, a behavior that results in an unpleasant event tends not to be repeated.

A good example of a dog learning the hard way is the dog who chases the house cat. He is told many times to leave the cat alone, yet he persists in teasing the cat. Then, one day he begins chasing the cat but the cat turns and swipes a claw across the dog's face, leaving him with a painful gash on his nose. The final result is that the dog stops chasing the cat.

HOW MANY TIMES A DAY?

AGE	RELIEF TRIPS
To 14 weeks	10
14–22 weeks	8
22–32 weeks	6
Adulthood	4
(dog stops growing)	

These are estimates, of course, but they are a guide to the *minimum* number of opportunities a dog should have each day to relieve himself.

TRAINING EQUIPMENT

COLLAR AND LEASH

For a Maltese, the collar and leash that you use for training must be one with which you are easily able to work, lightweight and perfectly safe.

TREATS

Have a bag of treats on hand. Something nutritious and easy to swallow works best. Use a soft treat, a chunk of cheese or a piece of cooked chicken rather than a dry biscuit. By the time the dog has finished chewing a dry treat, he will forget why he is being rewarded in the first place! By the way, using food rewards will not teach a dog to beg at the table—the only way to teach a dog to beg at the table is to give him food from the table. In training, rewarding the dog with a food treat will help him associate praise and the treats with learning new behaviors that obviously please his owner.

TRAINING BEGINS: ASK THE DOG A QUESTION

In order to teach your dog anything, you must first get his attention. After all, he cannot learn anything if he is looking away from you with his mind on something else.

To get his attention, ask him "School?" and immediately walk over to him and give him a treat as you tell him "Good dog." Wait a minute or two and repeat the routine, this time with a treat in your hand as you approach within a foot of the dog. Do not go directly to him, but stop about a foot short of him and hold out the treat as you ask "School?" He will see you approaching with a treat in your hand and most likely begin walking toward you. As you meet, give him the treat and praise again.

The third time, ask the question, have a treat in your hand and walk only a short distance toward the dog so that he must walk almost all the way to you. As he reaches you, give him the treat and praise again.

By this time, the dog will probably be getting the idea that if he pays attention to you, especially when you ask that question, it will pay off in treats and enjoyable activities for him. In other words, he learns that "school" means doing enjoyable things with you that result in treats and positive attention for him.

Remember that the dog does not understand your verbal language, he only recognizes sounds. Your question translates to a series of sounds for him, and those sounds become the signal to go to you and pay attention; if he does, he will get to interact with you plus receive treats and praise.

THE BASIC COMMANDS

TEACHING SIT

Now that you have the dog's attention, attach his leash and hold it in your left hand and a food treat in your right. Place your food hand at the dog's nose and let him lick the treat but not take it from you. Say "Sit" and slowly raise your food hand from in front of the dog's nose up over his head so that he is looking at the ceiling. As he bends his head upward, he will have to bend his knees to maintain his balance. As he bends his knees, he will assume a sit position. At that point, release the food treat and praise lavishly with comments such as "Good dog! Good sit!," etc. Remember to always praise

TRAINING RULES

If you want to be successful in training your dog, you have four rules to obey yourself:

1. Develop an understanding of how a dog thinks.
2. Do not blame the dog for lack of communication.
3. Define your dog's personality and act accordingly.
4. Have patience and be consistent.

enthusiastically, because dogs relish verbal praise from their owners and feel so proud of themselves whenever they accomplish a behavior.

You will not use food forever in getting the dog to obey your commands. Food is only used to teach new behaviors, and once the dog knows what you want when you give a specific command, you will wean him off the food treats but still maintain the verbal praise. After all, you will always have your voice with you, and there will be many times when you have no food rewards but expect the dog to obey.

PRACTICE MAKES PERFECT!
- Have training lessons with your dog every day in several short segments—three to five times a day for a few minutes at a time is ideal.
- Do not have long practice sessions. The dog will become easily bored.
- Never practice when you are tired, ill, worried or in an otherwise negative mood. This will transmit to the dog and may have an adverse effect on his performance.

Think fun, short and above all *positive*! End each session on a high note, rather than a failed exercise, and make sure to give a lot of praise. Enjoy the training and help your dog enjoy it, too.

TEACHING DOWN
Teaching the down exercise is easy when you understand how the dog perceives the down position, and it is very difficult when you do not. Dogs perceive the down position as a submissive one, therefore teaching the down exercise using a forceful method can sometimes make the dog develop such a fear of the down that he either runs away when you say "Down" or he attempts to snap at the person who tries to force him down.

Have the dog sit alongside your left leg, facing in the same direction as you are. Hold the leash in your left hand and a food treat in your right. Now place your left hand lightly on the top of the dog's shoulders where they meet above the spinal cord. Do not push down on the dog's shoulders; simply rest your left hand there so you

Train your Maltese using a light collar and leash. If you wish to progress to advanced off-leash exercises, only do so in a safely fenced area once the dog is reliably trained in the basic commands.

can guide the dog to lie down close to your left leg rather than to swing away from your side when he drops.

Now place the food hand at the dog's nose, say "Down" very softly (almost a whisper) and slowly lower the food hand to the dog's front feet. When the food hand reaches the floor, begin moving it forward along the floor in front of the dog. Keep talking softly to the dog, saying things like, "Do you want this treat? You can do this, good dog." Your reassuring tone of voice will help calm the dog as he tries to follow the food hand in order to get the treat.

When the dog's elbows touch the floor, release the food and praise softly. Try to get the dog to maintain that down position for several seconds before you let him sit up again. The goal here is to get the dog to settle down and not feel threatened in the down position.

TEACHING STAY
It is easy to teach the dog to stay in either a sit or a down position. Again, we use food and praise during the teaching process as we help the dog to understand exactly what it is that we are expecting him to do.

To teach the sit/stay, start with the dog sitting on your left side as before and hold the leash in your left hand. Have a food treat in your right hand and place your food hand at the dog's nose. Say "Stay" and step out on your right foot to stand directly in front of the dog, toe to toe, as he licks and nibbles the treat. Be sure to keep his head facing upward to maintain the sit position. Count to five and then swing around to stand next to the dog again with him on your left. As soon as you get back to the original position, release the food and praise lavishly.

To teach the down/stay, do the down as previously described. As soon as the dog lies down, say "Stay" and step out on your right foot just as you did in the sit/stay. Count to five and then return to stand beside the dog with him on your left side. Release the treat and praise as always.

Within a week to ten days, you can begin to add a bit of distance between you and your dog when you leave him. When you do, use your left hand open with the palm facing the dog as a stay signal, much the same as the hand signal a police officer uses to stop traffic at an intersection. Hold the food treat in your right hand as before, but this time the food is not touching the dog's nose. He will watch the food hand and quickly learn that he is going to get that treat as soon as you return to his side.

FEAR AGGRESSION

Pups who are subjected to physical abuse during training commonly end up with behavioral problems as adults. One common result of abuse is fear aggression, in which a dog will lash out, bare his teeth, snarl and finally bite someone by whom he feels threatened. For example, your daughter may be playing with the dog one afternoon. As they play hide-and-seek, she backs the dog into a corner and, as she attempts to tease him playfully, he bites her hand. Examine the cause of this behavior. Did your daughter ever hit the dog? Did someone who resembles your daughter hit or scream at the dog?

Fortunately, fear aggression is relatively easy to correct. Have your daughter engage in only positive activities with the dog, such as feeding, petting and walking. She should not give any corrections or negative feedback. If the dog still growls or cowers away from her, allow someone else to accompany them. After approximately one week, the dog should feel that he can rely on her for many positive things, and he will also be prevented from reacting fearfully towards anyone who might resemble her.

When you can stand 1 yard away from your dog for 30 seconds, you can then begin building time and distance in both stays. Eventually, the dog can be expected to remain in the stay position for prolonged periods of time until you return to him or call him to you. Always praise lavishly when he stays.

TEACHING COME

If you make teaching "come" a fun experience, you should never have a student that does not love the game or that fails to come when called. The secret, it seems, is never to use the word "come."

At times when an owner most wants his dog to come when called, the owner is likely upset or anxious and he allows these feelings to come through in the tone of his voice when he calls his dog. Hearing that desperation in his owner's voice, the dog fears the results of going to him and therefore either disobeys outright or runs in the opposite direction. The secret, therefore, is to teach the dog a game and, when you want him to come to you, simply play the game. It is practically a no-fail solution!

To begin, have several members of your family take a few food treats and each go into a different room in the house. Take turns calling the dog, and each person should celebrate the dog's finding him with a treat and lots of happy praise. When a person calls the dog, he is actually inviting the dog to find him and get a treat as a reward for "winning."

A few turns of the "Where are you?" game and the dog will understand that everyone is playing the game and that each person has a big celebration awaiting his success at locating him. Once he learns to love the game, simply calling out "Where are you?" will bring him running from wherever he is when he hears that all-important question.

The come command is recognized as one of the most important things to teach a dog, but there are trainers who work with

---

THE STUDENT'S STRESS TEST

During training sessions, you must be able to recognize signs of stress in your dog such as:

- tucking his tail between his legs
- lowering his head
- shivering or trembling
- standing completely still or running away
- panting and/or salivating
- avoiding eye contact
- flattening his ears back
- urinating submissively
- rolling over and lifting a leg
- grinning or baring teeth
- aggression when restrained

If your four-legged student displays these signs, he may just be nervous or intimidated. The training session may have been too lengthy, with not enough praise and affirmation. Stop for the day and try again tomorrow.

thousands of dogs and never teach the actual word "come." Yet these dogs will race to respond to a person who uses the dog's name followed by "Where are you?" For example, a woman has a 12-year-old companion dog who went blind, but who never fails to locate her owner when asked, "Where are you?"

Children particularly love to play this game with their dogs. Children can hide in smaller places like a shower or bathtub, behind a bed or under a table. The dog needs to work a little bit harder to find these hiding places, but, when he does, he loves to celebrate with a treat and a tussle with a favorite youngster.

TEACHING HEEL

Heeling means that the dog walks beside the owner without pulling. It takes time and patience on the owner's part to succeed at teaching the dog that he (the owner) will not proceed unless the dog is walking calmly beside him. Pulling out ahead on the leash is definitely not acceptable.

Begin with holding the leash in your left hand as the dog sits beside your left leg. Move the loop end of the leash to your right hand but keep your left hand short on the leash so it keeps the dog in close next to you.

HELPING PAWS

Your dog may not be the next Lassie, but every pet has the potential to do some tricks well. Identify his natural talents and hone them. Is your dog always happy and upbeat? Teach him to wag his tail or give you his paw on command. Real homebodies can be trained to do household chores, such as carrying a slipper or retrieving the weekday paper.

Say "Heel" and step forward on your left foot. Keep the dog close to you and take three steps. Stop and have the dog sit next to you in what we now call the heel position. Praise verbally, but do not touch the dog. Hesitate a moment and begin again with "Heel," taking three steps and stopping, at which point the dog is told to sit again.

Your goal here is to have the dog walk those three steps without pulling on the leash. When he will walk calmly beside you for three steps without pulling, increase the number of steps you take to five. When he will walk politely beside you while you take five steps, you can increase the length of your walk to ten steps. Keep increasing the length of your stroll until the dog will walk quietly beside you without pulling as long as you want him to heel. When you stop heeling, indicate to the dog that the exercise is over by verbally praising as you pet him and say "OK, good dog." The "OK" is used as a release word, meaning that the exercise is finished and the dog is free to relax.

If you are dealing with a dog who insists on tugging at the leash, simply "put on your brakes" and stand your ground until the dog realizes that the two of you are not going anywhere until he is beside you and moving at your pace, not his. It may take some time just standing there to convince the dog that you are the leader and you will be the one to decide on the direction and speed of your travel.

Each time the dog looks up at you or slows down to give a slack leash between the two of you, quietly praise him and say, "Good heel. Good dog." Eventually, the dog will begin to respond and within a few days

HEELING WELL

Teach your dog to heel in an enclosed area. Once you think the dog will obey reliably and you want to attempt advanced obedience exercises such as off-leash heeling, test him in a fenced-in area so he cannot run away.

he will be walking politely beside you without pulling on the leash. At first, the training sessions should be kept short and very positive; soon the dog will be able to walk nicely with you for increasingly longer distances. Remember also to give the dog free time and the opportunity to run and play when you have finished heel practice.

WEANING OFF FOOD IN TRAINING

Food is used in training new behaviors. Once the dog understands what behavior goes with a specific command, it is time to start weaning him off the food treats. At first, give a treat after each exercise. Then, start to give a treat only after every other exercise. Mix up the times when you offer a food reward and the times when you only offer praise so that the dog will never know when he is going to receive both food and praise and when he is going to receive only praise. This is called a variable ratio reward system and it proves successful because there is always the chance that the owner will produce a treat, so the dog never stops trying for that reward. No matter what, *always* give verbal praise.

OBEDIENCE CLASSES

It is a good idea to enroll in an obedience class if one is avail-

FAMILY TIES

If you have other pets in the home and/or interact often with the pets of friends and other family members, your pup will respond to those pets in much the same manner as you do. It is only when you show fear of or resentment toward another animal that he will act fearful or unfriendly.

able in your area. If yours is a show dog, show-handling classes would be more appropriate. Many areas have dog clubs that offer basic obedience training as well as preparatory classes for obedience competi-

tion. There are also local dog trainers who offer similar classes.

At obedience trials, dogs can earn titles at various levels of competition. The beginning levels of competition include basic behaviors such as sit, down, heel, etc. The more advanced levels of competition include jumping, retrieving, scent discrimination and signal work. The advanced levels require a dog and owner to put a lot of time and effort into their training, and the titles that can be earned at these levels of competition are very prestigious.

Your Maltese should never fail to come running when you call him. Aside from just obeying a command, he should be happy to see you!

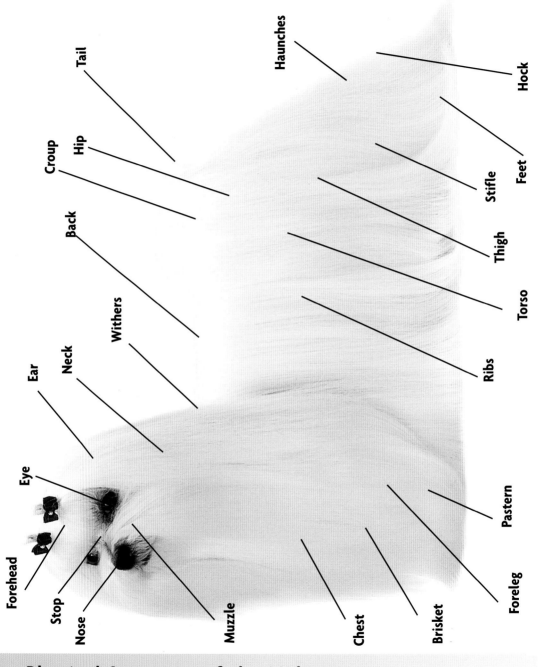

Physical Structure of the Maltese

MALTESE

Dogs suffer from many of the same physical illnesses as people. They might even share many of the same psychological problems. Since people usually know more about human diseases than canine maladies, many of the terms used in this chapter will be familiar but not necessarily those used by veterinarians. We will use the term *x-ray*, instead of the more acceptable term *radiograph*. We will also use the familiar term *symptoms* even though dogs don't have symptoms, which are verbal descriptions of the patient's feelings; dogs have *clinical signs*. Since dogs can't speak, we have to look for clinical signs...but we still use the term *symptoms* in this book.

As a general rule, medicine is practiced. That term is not arbitrary. Medicine is a constantly changing art as we learn more and more about genetics, electronic aids (like CAT scans and MRIs) and daily laboratory advances. There are many dog maladies, like canine hip dysplasia, which are not universally treated in the same manner.

Before you buy a dog, meet and interview the vets in your area. Take everything into consideration; discuss background, specialties, fees, emergency policies, etc.

Some vets opt for surgery more often than others do.

SELECTING A QUALIFIED VET
Your selection of a veterinarian should be based upon personality and skill with small dogs as well as his convenience to your home. You want a veterinarian who is close because you might have emergencies or need to make multiple visits for treatments. You want a vet who has services that you might require such as boarding and grooming facilities, as well as pet supplies and a good reputation for ability and responsiveness. There is

Recognizing a Sick Dog

Unlike colicky babies and cranky children, our canine kids cannot tell us when they are feeling ill. Therefore, there are a number of signs that owners can identify to know that their dogs are not feeling well.

Take note for physical manifestations such as:

- unusual, bad odor, including bad breath
- excessive shedding
- wax in the ears, chronic ear irritation
- oily, flaky, dull haircoat
- mucus, tearing or similar discharge in the eyes
- fleas or mites
- mucus in stool, diarrhea
- sensitivity to petting or handling
- licking at paws, scratching face, etc.

Keep an eye out for behavioral changes as well including:

- lethargy, idleness
- lack of patience or general irritability
- lack of appetite
- phobias (fear of people, loud noises, etc.)
- strange behavior, suspicion, fear
- coprophagia
- more frequent barking
- whimpering, crying

Get Well Soon

You don't need a DVM to provide good TLC to your sick or recovering dog, but you do need to pay attention to some details that normally wouldn't bother him. The following tips will aid Fido's recovery and get him back on his paws again:

- Keep his space free of irritating smells, like heavy perfumes and air fresheners.
- Rest is the best medicine! Avoid harsh lighting that will prevent your dog from sleeping. Shade him from bright sunlight during the day and dim the lights in the evening.
- Keep the noise level down. Animals are more sensitive to sound when they are sick.

- Be attentive to any necessary temperature adjustments. A dog with a fever needs a cool room and cold liquids. A bitch that is whelping or recovering from surgery will be more comfortable in a warm room, consuming warm liquids and food.
- You wouldn't send a sick child back to school early, so don't rush your dog back into a full routine until he seems absolutely ready.

nothing more frustrating than having to wait a day or more to get a response from your veterinarian.

All veterinarians are licensed and their diplomas and/or certificates should be displayed in their waiting rooms. There are, however, many veterinary specialties that usually require further studies and internships. There are specialists in heart problems (veterinary cardiologists), skin problems (veterinary dermatologists), teeth and gum problems (veterinary dentists), eye problems (veterinary ophthalmologists) and x-rays (veterinary radiologists), as well as surgeons who have specialties in bones, muscles or certain organs. Most veterinarians do routine surgery such as neutering, stitching up wounds and docking tails for those breeds in which such is required for show purposes. When the problem affecting your dog is serious, it is not unusual or impudent to get another medical opinion, although it is always courteous

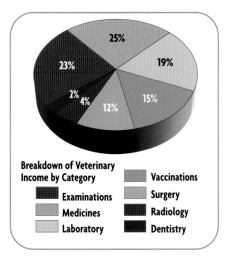

A typical vet's income, categorized according to services provided. This survey dealt with small-animal practices.

Breakdown of Veterinary Income by Category

- Examinations
- Medicines
- Laboratory
- Vaccinations
- Surgery
- Radiology
- Dentistry

to advise the vets concerned about this. You might also want to compare costs among several veterinarians. Sophisticated health care and veterinary services can be very costly. Don't be bashful about discussing these costs with your veterinarian or his staff. Important decisions are often based upon financial considerations.

PREVENTATIVE MEDICINE
It is much easier, less costly and more effective to practice preventative medicine than to fight bouts of illness and disease. Properly bred puppies come from parents that were selected based upon their genetic-disease profiles. Their dam should have been vaccinated, free of all internal and external parasites and properly nourished. For these reasons, a

NEUTERING/SPAYING
Male dogs are neutered. The operation removes the testicles and requires that the dog be anesthetized. Recovery takes about one week. Females are spayed. This is major surgery and it usually takes a bitch two weeks to recover.

A SKUNKY PROBLEM

Have you noticed your dog dragging his rump along the floor? If so, it is likely that his anal sacs are impacted or possibly infected. The anal sacs are small pouches located on both sides of the anus under the skin and muscles. They are about the size and shape of a grape and contain a foul-smelling liquid. Their contents are usually emptied when the dog has a bowel movement but, if not emptied completely, they will impact, which will cause your dog much pain. Fortunately, your veterinarian can tend to this problem easily by draining the sacs for the dog. Be aware that your dog might also empty his anal sacs in cases of extreme fright.

visit to the veterinarian who cared for the dam is recommended. The dam can pass on disease resistance to her puppies, which can last for eight to ten weeks. She can also pass on parasites and many infections. That's why you should learn as much as possible about the dam's health.

WEANING TO FIVE MONTHS OLD
Puppies should be weaned by the time they are about two months old. A puppy that remains for at least eight weeks with his mother and littermates usually adapts better to other dogs and people later in life.

Some new owners have their puppy examined by a veterinarian immediately, which is a good idea. Vaccination programs usually begin when the puppy is very young. The puppy will have his teeth examined and have his skeletal conformation and general health checked prior to certification by the veterinarian. Puppies in certain breeds have problems with their kneecaps, cataracts and other eye problems, heart murmurs and undescended testicles. They may also have personality problems and your veterinarian might have training in temperament evaluation.

VACCINATION SCHEDULING
Most vaccinations are given by injection and should only be done by a veterinarian. Both he and you should keep a record of the date of the injection, the identification of the vaccine and the amount given. Some vets give a first vaccination at eight weeks, but most dog breeders prefer the course not to commence until about ten weeks because of negating any antibodies passed on by the dam. The vaccination scheduling is usually based on a 15-day cycle. You must take your vet's advice as to when to vaccinate, as this may differ according to the vaccine used. Most vaccinations immunize your puppy against viruses.

The usual vaccines contain immunizing doses of several different viruses such as distemper, parvovirus, parainfluenza and hepatitis. There are other vaccines available when the puppy is at risk. You should rely upon professional advice. This is especially true for the booster-shot program. Most vaccination programs require a booster when the puppy is a year old and once a year thereafter. In some cases,

"P" STANDS FOR PROBLEM

Urinary tract disease is a serious condition that requires immediate medical attention. Symptoms include urinating in inappropriate places or the need to urinate frequently in small amounts. Urinary-tract disease is most effectively treated with antibiotics. To help promote good urinary-tract health, owners must always be sure that a constant supply of fresh water is available to their pets.

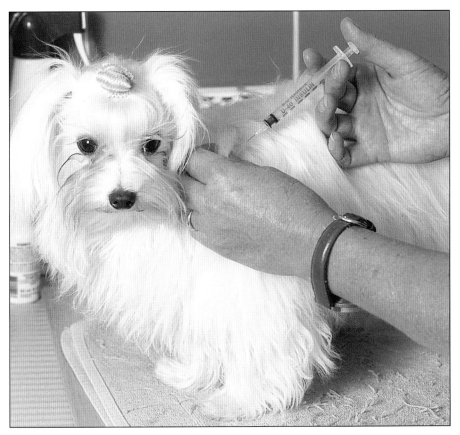

Your Maltese will receive most of his vaccinations in puppyhood, and then receive annual booster shots.

HEALTH AND VACCINATION SCHEDULE

Age in Weeks:	6th	8th	10th	12th	14th	16th	20-24th	52nd
Worm Control	✔	✔	✔	✔	✔	✔	✔	
Neutering							✔	
Heartworm		✔		✔		✔	✔	
Parvovirus	✔		✔		✔		✔	✔
Distemper		✔		✔		✔		✔
Hepatitis		✔		✔		✔		✔
Leptospirosis								✔
Parainfluenza	✔		✔		✔			✔
Dental Examination		✔					✔	✔
Complete Physical		✔					✔	✔
Coronavirus				✔			✔	✔
Canine Cough	✔							
Hip Dysplasia							✔	
Rabies							✔	

Vaccinations are not instantly effective. It takes about two weeks for the dog's immune system to develop antibodies. Most vaccinations require annual booster shots. Your veterinarian should guide you in this regard.

circumstances may require more or less frequent immunizations.

Canine cough, more formally known as tracheobronchitis, is treated with a vaccine that is sprayed into the dog's nostrils. Canine cough is usually included in routine vaccination, but this is often not as effective as for other major diseases.

FIVE TO TWELVE MONTHS OF AGE
Unless you intend to breed or show your dog, neutering the puppy around six months of age is recommended. Discuss this with your veterinarian. Neutering has proven to be extremely beneficial to both male and female puppies. Besides eliminating the possibility of pregnancy and pyometra in bitches and testicular cancer in males, it inhibits (but does not prevent) breast cancer in bitches and prostate cancer in male dogs.

Your veterinarian should provide your puppy with a thorough dental evaluation at six months of age, ascertaining whether all the permanent teeth

First Aid at a Glance

Burns
Place the affected area under cool water; use ice if only a small area is burnt.

Bee stings/Insect bites
Apply ice to relieve swelling; antihistamine dosed properly.

Animal bites
Clean any bleeding area; apply pressure until bleeding subsides; go to the vet.

Spider bites
Use cold compress and a pressurized pack to inhibit venom's spreading.

Antifreeze poisoning
Induce vomiting with hydrogen peroxide. Seek *immediate* veterinary help!

Fish hooks
Removal best handled by vet; hook must be cut in order to remove.

Snake bites
Pack ice around bite; contact vet quickly; identify snake for proper antivenin.

Car accident
Move dog from roadway with blanket; seek veterinary aid.

Shock
Calm the dog, keep him warm; seek immediate veterinary help.

Nosebleed
Apply cold compress to the nose; apply pressure to any visible abrasion.

Bleeding
Apply pressure above the area; treat wound by applying a cotton pack.

Heat stroke
Submerge dog in cold bath; cool down with fresh air and water; go to the vet.

Frostbite/Hypothermia
Warm the dog with a warm bath, electric blankets or hot water bottles.

Abrasions
Clean the wound and wash out thoroughly with fresh water; apply antiseptic.

!! *Remember: an injured dog may attempt to bite a helping hand from fear and confusion. Always muzzle the dog before trying to offer assistance.* !!

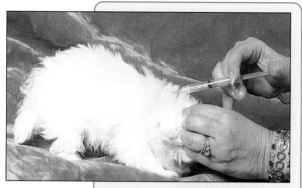

PUPPY VACCINATIONS
Your veterinarian will probably recommend that your puppy be fully vaccinated before you take him outside. There are airborne diseases, parasite eggs in the grass and unexpected visits from other dogs that might be dangerous to your puppy's health.

have erupted properly. A home dental-care regimen should be initiated at six months, including brushing weekly and providing good dental devices (such as nylon bones). Regular dental care promotes healthy teeth, fresh breath and a longer life.

OVER ONE YEAR OF AGE
Once a year, your grown dog should visit the vet for an examination and vaccination boosters. Some vets recommend blood tests, thyroid-level check and dental evaluation to accompany these annual visits. A thorough clinical evaluation by the vet can provide critical back-ground information for your dog. Blood tests are often performed at one year of age, and dental examinations around the third or fourth birthday. In the long run, quality preventative care for your pet can save money, teeth and lives.

SKIN PROBLEMS IN MALTESE
Veterinarians are consulted by dog owners for skin problems more than for any other group of diseases or maladies. Dogs' skin is almost as sensitive as humans' skin and both suffer almost the same ailments (though the occurrence of acne in most breeds is rare!). For this reason, veterinary dermatology has developed into a specialty practiced by many veterinarians.

Since many skin problems have visual symptoms that are almost identical, it requires the skill of an experienced veterinary dermatologist to identify and cure many of the more severe skin disorders. Pet shops sell many treatments for skin problems but most of the treatments are directed at symptoms and not the underlying problem(s). If your dog is suffering from a skin disorder, you should seek professional assistance as quickly as possible. As with all diseases, the earlier a problem is identified and treated, the more successful can be the cure.

HEREDITARY SKIN DISORDERS
Veterinary dermatologists are currently researching a number of skin disorders that are believed to have a hereditary basis. These inherited diseases are transmitted by both parents, who appear (phenotypically) normal but have a recessive gene for the disease, meaning that they carry, but are not affected by, the disease. These diseases pose serious problems to breeders because in some instances there is no method of identifying carriers. Often the secondary diseases associated with these skin conditions are even more debilitating than the disorder itself, including cancers and respiratory problems.

Among the hereditary skin disorders, for which the mode of inheritance is known, are acrodermatitis, cutaneous asthenia (Ehlers-Danlos syndrome), sebaceous adenitis, cyclic hematopoiesis, dermatomyositis, IgA deficiency, color dilution alopecia and nodular dermatofibrosis. Some of these disorders are limited to one or two breeds and others affect a large number of breeds. All inherited diseases must be diagnosed and treated by a veterinary specialist.

PARASITE BITES
Many of us are allergic to insect bites. The bites itch, erupt and may even become infected. Dogs have the same reaction to fleas, ticks and/or mites. When an insect lands on you, you have the chance to whisk it away with your hand. Unfortunately, when your dog is bitten by a flea, tick or mite, he can only scratch it away or bite it. By the time the dog has been bitten, the parasite has done some of its damage. It may also have laid eggs to cause further problems in the near future. The itching from parasite bites is probably due to the saliva injected into the site when the parasite sucks the dog's blood.

AUTO-IMMUNE SKIN CONDITIONS
Auto-immune skin conditions are commonly referred to as

KNOW WHEN TO POSTPONE A VACCINATION

While the visit to the vet is costly, it is never advisable to update a vaccination when visiting with a sick or pregnant dog. Vaccinations also should be avoided for all elderly dogs. If your dog is showing the signs of any illness or any medical condition, no matter how serious or mild, including skin irritations, do not vaccinate. Likewise, a lame dog should never be vaccinated; any dog undergoing surgery or on any immunosuppressant drugs should not be vaccinated until fully recovered.

being allergic to yourself, while allergies are usually inflammatory reactions to an outside stimulus. Auto-immune diseases cause serious damage to the tissues that are involved.

The best known auto-immune disease is lupus, which affects people as well as dogs. The symptoms are variable and may affect the kidneys, bones, blood chemistry and skin. It can be fatal to both dogs and humans, though it is not thought to be transmissible. It is

VACCINE ALLERGIES
Vaccines do not work all the time. Sometimes dogs are allergic to them and many times the antibodies, which are supposed to be stimulated by the vaccine, just are not produced. You should keep your dog in the veterinary clinic for an hour after he is vaccinated to be sure he does not experience any allergic reactions.

DISEASE REFERENCE CHART

	What is it?	What causes it?	Symptoms
Leptospirosis	Severe disease that affects the internal organs; can be spread to people.	A bacterium, which is often carried by rodents, that enters through mucous membranes and spreads quickly throughout the body.	Range from fever, vomiting and loss of appetite in less severe cases to shock, irreversible kidney damage and possibly death in most severe cases.
Rabies	Potentially deadly virus that infects warm-blooded mammals.	Bite from a carrier of the virus, mainly wild animals.	1st stage: dog exhibits change in behavior, fear. 2nd stage: dog's behavior becomes more aggressive. 3rd stage: loss of coordination, trouble with bodily functions.
Parvovirus	Highly contagious virus, potentially deadly.	Ingestion of the virus, which is usually spread through the feces of infected dogs.	Most common: severe diarrhea. Also vomiting, fatigue, lack of appetite.
Kennel cough	Contagious respiratory infection.	Combination of types of bacteria and virus. Most common: *Bordetella bronchiseptica* bacteria and parainfluenza virus.	Chronic cough.
Distemper	Disease primarily affecting respiratory and nervous system.	Virus that is related to the human measles virus.	Mild symptoms such as fever, lack of appetite and mucus secretion progress to evidence of brain damage, "hard pad."
Hepatitis	Virus primarily affecting the liver.	Canine adenovirus type I (CAV-1). Enters system when dog breathes in particles.	Lesser symptoms include listlessness, diarrhea, vomiting. More severe symptoms include "blue-eye" (clumps of virus in eye).
Coronavirus	Virus resulting in digestive problems.	Virus is spread through infected dog's feces.	Stomach upset evidenced by lack of appetite, vomiting, diarrhea.

usually successfully treated with cortisone, prednisone or similar corticosteroid, but extensive use of these drugs can have harmful side effects.

AIRBORNE ALLERGIES

Just as humans have hay fever, rose fever and other fevers from which they suffer during the pollinating season, many dogs suffer from the same allergies. When the pollen count is high, your dog might suffer but don't expect him to sneeze and have a runny nose as a human would. Dogs react to pollen allergies the same way they react to fleas—they scratch and bite themselves.

Dogs, like humans, can be tested for allergens. Discuss the testing with your veterinary dermatologist.

SKIN ALLERGIES

Like many other breeds, some Maltese are prone to allergies, but these can often be kept under control with a carefully considered diet. The allergy might be noticed as "hot spots" on the skin, despite there being no sign of external parasites. A low-protein diet often seems to suit skin troubles, and ideally one should try to identify and eliminate any foods that are causing or exacerbating the problem.

Indeed it is often extremely difficult to ascertain the cause of the allergy. There are many possibilities, ranging from the sitting room carpet, the shampoo used when bathing and, quite frequently, certain grasses and molds. In cases of skin allergy, it is a good idea to change shampoo, conditioning rinse and any other coat sprays used, for these are perhaps the easiest items to eliminate before looking further if necessary. It goes without saying that your Maltese must be kept free of external parasites such as fleas.

PET ADVANTAGES

If you do not intend to show or breed your new puppy, your veterinarian will probably recommend that you spay your female or neuter your male. Some people believe neutering leads to weight gain, but if you feed and exercise your dog properly, this is easily avoided. Spaying or neutering can actually have many positive outcomes, such as:

• training becomes easier, as the dog focuses less on the urge to mate and more on you!

• females are protected from unplanned pregnancy as well as ovarian and uterine cancers.

• males are guarded from testicular tumors and have a reduced risk of developing prostate cancer.

Talk to your vet regarding the right age to spay/neuter and other aspects of the procedure.

FOOD PROBLEMS

FOOD ALLERGIES

Some dogs are allergic to many foods that are best-sellers and highly recommended by breeders and veterinarians. Changing the brand of food that you buy may not eliminate the problem if the element to which the dog is allergic is contained in the new brand.

Recognizing a food allergy is difficult. Humans vomit or have rashes when they eat a food to which they are allergic. Dogs

The Eyes Have It!

Eye disease is more prevalent among dogs than most people think, ranging from slight infections that are easily treated to serious complications that can lead to permanent sight loss. Eye diseases need veterinary attention in their early stages to prevent irreparable damage. This list provides descriptions of some common eye diseases:

Cataracts: Symptoms are white or gray discoloration of the eye lens and pupil, which causes fuzzy or completely obscured vision. Surgical treatment is required to remove the damaged lens and replace it with an artificial one.

Conjunctivitis: An inflammation of the mucous membrane that lines the eye socket, leaving the eyes red and puffy with excessive discharge. This condition is easily treated with antibiotics.

Corneal damage: The cornea is the transparent covering of the iris and pupil. Injuries are difficult to detect, but manifest themselves in surface abnormality, redness, pain and discharge. Most infections of the cornea are treated with antibiotics and require immediate medical attention.

Dry eye: This condition is caused by deficient production of tears that lubricate and protect the eye surface. A telltale sign is yellow-green discharge. Left undiagnosed, your dog will experience considerable pain, infections and possibly blindness. Dry eye is commonly treated with antibiotics, although more advanced cases may require surgery.

Glaucoma: This is caused by excessive fluid pressure in the eye. Symptoms are red eyes, gray or blue discoloration, pain, enlarged eyeballs and loss of vision. Antibiotics sometimes help, but surgery may be needed.

neither vomit nor (usually) develop a rash. They react in the same manner as they do to an airborne or flea allergy: they itch, scratch and bite, thus making the diagnosis extremely difficult. While pollen allergies and parasite bites are usually seasonal, food allergies are year-round problems.

FOOD INTOLERANCE

Food intolerance is the inability of the dog to completely digest certain foods. For example, puppies that may have done very well on their mother's milk may not do well on cow's milk. The result of this food intolerance may be loose bowels, passing gas and stomach pains. These are the only obvious symptoms of food intolerance and that makes the diagnosis difficult.

TREATING FOOD PROBLEMS

It is possible to handle food allergies and food intolerance yourself. Put your dog on a diet that he has never had. Obviously, if he has never eaten this new food, he can't yet have been allergic or intolerant of it. Start with a single ingredient that is not in the dog's diet at the present time. Ingredients like chopped beef or chicken are common in dogs' diets, so try something more exotic like fish, rabbit or another source of qual-

DENTAL HEALTH

A dental examination is in order when the dog is between six months and one year of age so that any permanent teeth that have erupted incorrectly can be corrected. It is important to begin a brushing routine at home, using dental-care products made for dogs, such as a small toothbrush and canine toothpaste. Durable nylon and safe edible chews should be a part of your puppy's arsenal for good health, good teeth and pleasant breath. The vast majority of dogs three to four years old and older has diseases of the gums from lack of dental attention. Using the various types of dental chews can be very effective in controling dental plaque.

ity animal protein. Keep the dog on this diet (with no additives) for a month. If the symptoms of food allergy or intolerance disappear, chances are your dog has a food allergy.

Don't think that the single ingredient cured the problem. You still must find a suitable diet and ascertain which ingredient in the old diet was objectionable. This is most easily done by adding ingredients to the new diet one at a time. Let the dog stay on the modified diet for a month before you add another ingredient. Eventually, you will determine the ingredient that caused the adverse reaction.

An alternative method is to carefully study the ingredients in the diet to which your dog is allergic or intolerant. Identify the main ingredient in this diet and eliminate the main ingredient by buying a different food that does not have that ingredient. Keep experimenting until the symptoms disappear after one month on the new diet. Always remain in touch with your vet.

Don't Eat the Daisies!

Many plants and flowers are beautiful to look at, but can be highly toxic if ingested by your dog. Reactions range from abdominal pain and vomiting to convulsions and death. If the following plants are in your home, remove them. If they are outside your house or in your yard, avoid accidents by making sure your dog is never left unsupervised in those locations.

Azalea
Belladonna
Bird of paradise
Bulbs
Calla lily
Cardinal flower
Castor bean
Chinaberry tree
Daphne

Dumb cane
Dutchman's breeches
Elephant's ear
Hydrangea
Jack-in-the-pulpit
Jasmine
Jimsonweed
Larkspur
Laurel
Lily of the valley

Mescal bean
Mushrooms
Nightshade
Philodendron
Poinsettia
Prunus species
Tobacco
Yellow jasmine
Yews, *Taxus* species

Always supervise your Maltese outdoors and be careful of where he roams. A variety of plants are poisonous to dogs, and the Maltese's abundant coat makes it easy for him to pick up parasites, sharp grass seeds and other irritants.

A male dog flea, *Ctenocephalides canis.*

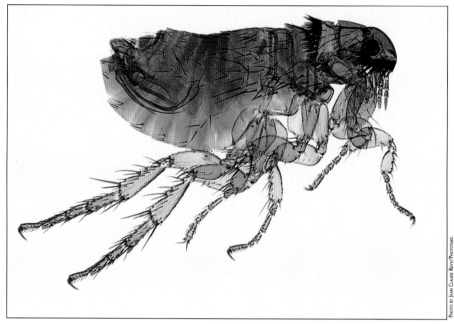

Photo by Jean Claude Revy/Phototake.

EXTERNAL PARASITES

FLEAS

Of all the problems to which dogs are prone, none is more well known and frustrating than fleas. Flea infestation is relatively simple to cure but difficult to prevent. Parasites that are harbored inside the body are a bit more difficult to eradicate but they are easier to control.

To control flea infestation, you have to understand the flea's life cycle. Fleas are often thought of as a summertime problem, but centrally heated homes have changed the patterns and fleas can be found at any time of the year. The most effective method of flea control is a two-stage approach: one stage to kill the adult fleas, and the other to control the development of pre-adult fleas. Unfortunately, no single active ingredient is effective against all stages of the life cycle.

FLEA KILLER CAUTION— "POISON"

Flea-killers are poisonous. You should not spray these toxic chemicals on areas of a dog's body that he licks, including his genitals and his face. Flea killers taken internally are a better answer, but check with your vet in case internal therapy is not advised for your dog.

LIFE CYCLE STAGES

During its life, a flea will pass through four life stages: egg, larva, pupa or nymph and adult. The adult stage is the most visible and irritating stage of the flea life cycle, and this is why the majority of flea-control products concentrate on this stage. The fact is that adult fleas account for only 1% of the total flea population, and the other 99% exist in pre-adult stages, i.e., eggs, larvae and nymphs. The pre-adult stages are barely visible to the naked eye.

THE LIFE CYCLE OF THE FLEA

Eggs are laid on the dog, usually in quantities of about 20 or 30, several times a day. The adult female flea must have a blood meal before each egg-laying session. When first laid, the eggs will cling to the dog's hair, as the eggs are still moist. However, they will quickly dry out and fall from the dog, especially if the dog moves around or scratches. Many eggs will fall off in the dog's favorite area or an area in which he spends a lot of time, such as his bed.

Once the eggs fall from the dog onto the carpet or furniture, they will hatch into larvae. This takes from one to ten days. Larvae are not particularly mobile and will usually travel only a few inches from where they hatch. However, they do have a tendency to move away from bright light and heavy

> ### EN GARDE:
> ### CATCHING FLEAS OFF GUARD!
> Consider the following ways to arm yourself against fleas:
> - Add a small amount of pennyroyal or eucalyptus oil to your dog's bath. These natural remedies repel fleas.
> - Supplement your dog's food with fresh garlic (minced or grated) and a hearty amount of brewer's yeast, both of which ward off fleas.
> - Use a flea comb on your dog daily. Submerge fleas in a cup of bleach to kill them quickly.
> - Confine the dog to only a few rooms to limit the spread of fleas in the home.
> - Vacuum daily...and get all of the crevices! Dispose of the bag every few days until the problem is under control.
> - Wash your dog's bedding daily. Cover cushions where your dog sleeps with towels, and wash the towels often.

traffic—under furniture and behind doors are common places to find high quantities of flea larvae.

The flea larvae feed on dead organic matter, including adult flea feces, until they are ready to change into adult fleas. Fleas will usually remain as larvae for around seven days. After this period, the larvae will pupate into protective pupae. While inside the pupae, the larvae will undergo metamorphosis and change into adult fleas. This can take as little time as a few days, but the adult fleas can remain inside the pupae waiting to hatch for up to two years. The pupae are signaled to hatch by certain stimuli, such as physical pressure—the pupae's being stepped on, heat from an animal's lying on the pupae or increased carbon-dioxide levels and vibrations—indicating that a suitable host is available.

Once hatched, the adult flea must feed within a few days. Once the adult flea finds a host, it will not leave voluntarily. It only becomes dislodged by grooming or the host animal's scratching.

The adult flea will remain on the host for the duration of its life unless forcibly removed.

TREATING THE ENVIRONMENT AND THE DOG

Treating fleas should be a two-pronged attack. First, the environment needs to be treated; this includes carpets and furniture, especially the dog's bedding and areas underneath furniture. The environment should be treated with a household spray containing an Insect Growth Regulator (IGR) and an insecticide to kill the adult fleas. Most IGRs are effective against eggs and larvae; they actually mimic the fleas' own hormones and stop the eggs and larvae from developing into adult fleas. There are currently no treatments available to attack the pupa stage of the life cycle, so the adult insecticide is used to kill the newly hatched adult fleas before they find a host. Most IGRs are active for many months, while

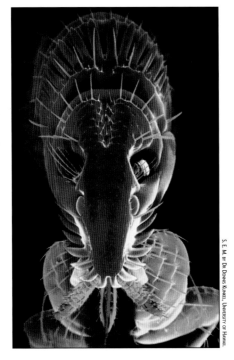

A scanning electron micrograph of a dog or cat flea, *Ctenocephalides*, magnified more than 100x. This image has been colorized for effect.

THE LIFE CYCLE OF THE FLEA

Adult

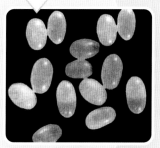

Egg

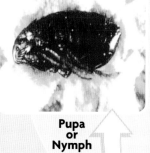

**Pupa
or
Nymph**

Larva

A LOOK AT FLEAS

Fleas have been around for millions of years and have adapted to changing host animals. They are able to go through a complete life cycle in less than one month or they can extend their lives to almost two years by remaining as pupae or cocoons. They do not need blood or any other food for up to 20 months.

INSECT GROWTH REGULATOR (IGR)

Two types of products should be used when treating fleas—a product to treat the pet and a product to treat the home. Adult fleas represent less than 1% of the flea population. The pre-adult fleas (eggs, larvae and pupae) represent more than 99% of the flea population and are found in the environment; it is in the case of pre-adult fleas that products containing an Insect Growth Regulator (IGR) should be used in the home.

IGRs are a new class of compounds used to prevent the development of insects. They do not kill the insect outright, but instead use the insect's biology against it to stop it from completing its growth. Products that contain methoprene are the world's first and leading IGRs. Used to control fleas and other insects, this type of IGR will stop flea larvae from developing and protect the house for up to seven months.

adult insecticides are only active for a few days.

When treating with a household spray, it is a good idea to vacuum before applying the product. This stimulates as many pupae as possible to hatch into adult fleas. The vacuum cleaner should also be treated with an insecticide to prevent the eggs and larvae that have been collected in the vacuum bag from hatching.

The second stage of treatment is to apply an adult insecticide to the dog. Traditionally, this would be in the form of a collar or a spray, but more recent innovations include digestible insecticides that poison the fleas when they ingest the dog's blood. Alternatively, there are drops that, when placed on the back of the dog's neck, spread throughout the hair and skin to kill adult fleas.

TICKS

Though not as common as fleas, ticks are found all over the tropical and temperate world. They don't bite, like fleas; they harpoon. They dig their sharp proboscis (nose) into the dog's skin and drink the blood. Their

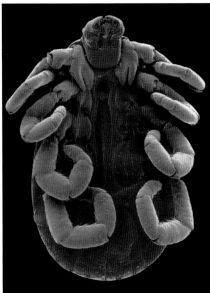

S. E. M. BY DR. DENNIS KUNKEL, UNIVERSITY OF HAWAII.

only food and drink is dog's blood. Dogs can get Lyme disease, Rocky Mountain spotted fever, tick bite paralysis and many other diseases from ticks. They may live where fleas are found and they like to hide in cracks or seams in walls. They are controlled the same way fleas are controlled.

The American dog tick, *Dermacentor variabilis*, may well be the most common dog tick in many geographical areas, especially those areas where the climate is hot and humid. Most dog ticks have life expectancies of a week to six months, depending upon climatic conditions. They can neither jump nor fly, but they can crawl slowly and can range up to 16 feet to reach a sleeping or unsuspecting dog.

MITES

Just as fleas and ticks can be problematic for your dog, mites can also lead to an itchy nuisance. Microscopic in size, mites are related to ticks and generally take up permanent residence on their host animal— in this case, your dog! The term *mange* refers to any infestation caused by one of the mighty mites, of which there are six varieties that concern dog owners.

Demodex mites cause a condition known as demodicosis

DEER-TICK CROSSING

The great outdoors may be fun for your dog, but it also is a home to dangerous ticks. Deer ticks carry a bacterium known as *Borrelia burgdorferi* and are most active in the autumn and spring. When infections are caught early, penicillin and tetracycline are effective antibiotics, but if left untreated the bacteria may cause neurological, kidney and cardiac problems as well as long-term trouble with walking and painful joints.

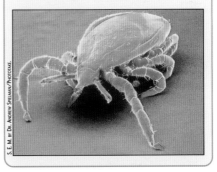

S. E. M. BY DR. ANDREW SPIELMAN/PHOTOTAKE.

PHOTO BY DR. DENNIS KUNKEL, UNIVERSITY OF HAWAII.

The head of an American dog tick, *Dermacentor variabilis*, enlarged and colorized for effect.

The mange mite, *Psoroptes bovis*, can infest cattle and other domestic animals.

PHOTO BY JAMES HAYDEN/YOAV/PHOTOTAKE.

(sometimes called red mange or follicular mange), in which the mites live in the dog's hair follicles and sebaceous glands in larger-than-normal amounts. This type of mange is commonly passed from the dam to her puppies and usually shows up on the puppies' muzzles, though demodicosis is not transferable from one normal dog to another. Most dogs recover from this type of mange without any treatment, though topical therapies are commonly prescribed by the vet.

Human lice look like dog lice; the two are closely related.

PHOTO BY DWIGHT R. KUHN.

The *Cheyletiellosis* mite is the hook-mouthed culprit associated with "walking dandruff," a condition that affects dogs as well as cats and rabbits. This mite lives on the surface of the animal's skin and is readily transferable through direct or indirect contact with an affected animal. The dandruff is present in the form of scaly skin, which may or may not be itchy. If not treated, this mange can affect a whole kennel of dogs and can be spread to humans as well.

The *Sarcoptes* mite causes intense itching on the dog in the form of a condition known as scabies or sarcoptic mange. The cycle of the *Sarcoptes* mite lasts about three weeks, and the mites live in the top layer of the dog's skin (epidermis), preferably in areas with little hair. Scabies is highly contagious and can be passed to humans. Sometimes an allergic reaction to the mite worsens the severe itching associated with sarcoptic mange.

Ear mites, *Otodectes cynotis,* lead to otodectic mange, which most commonly affects the outer ear canal of the dog, though other areas can be affected as well. Dogs with ear-mite infestation commonly scratch at their ears, causing further irritation, and shake their heads. Dark brown droppings in the outer ear confirm the diagnosis. Your vet can prescribe a treatment to flush out the ears and kill any eggs in the ears. A complete month of treatment is necessary to cure the mange.

Two other mites, less common in dogs, include *Dermanyssus gallinae* (the poultry or red mite) and *Eutrombicula alfreddugesi* (the North American mite associated with trombiculidiasis or chigger infestation). The poultry mite frequently lives on chickens, but can transfer to dogs who spend time near farm animals. Chigger infestation affects dogs in the

NOT A DROP TO DRINK
Never allow your dog to swim in polluted water or public areas where water quality can be suspect. Even perfectly clear water can harbor parasites, many of which can cause serious to fatal illnesses in canines. Areas inhabited by water-fowl and other wildlife are especially dangerous.

Central US who have exposure to woodlands. The types of mange caused by both of these mites are treatable by veterinarians.

INTERNAL PARASITES
Most animals—fishes, birds and mammals, including dogs and humans—have worms and other parasites that live inside their bodies. According to Dr. Herbert R. Axelrod, the fish pathologist, there are two kinds of parasites: dumb and smart. The smart parasites live in peaceful cooperation with their hosts (symbiosis), while the dumb parasites kill their hosts. Most worm infections are relatively easy to control. If they are not controlled, they weaken the host dog to the point that other medical problems occur, but they do not kill the host as dumb parasites would.

A brown dog tick, *Rhipicephalus sanguineus*, is an uncommon but annoying tick found on dogs.

DO NOT MIX
Never mix parasite-control products without first consulting your vet. Some products can become toxic when combined with others and can cause fatal consequences.

The roundworm *Rhabditis* can infect both dogs and humans.

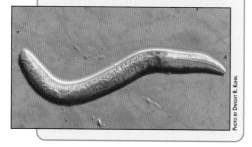

The roundworm, *Ascaris lumbricoides.*

ROUNDWORMS

Average-size dogs can pass 1,360,000 roundworm eggs every day. For example, if there were only 1 million dogs in the world, the world would be saturated with thousands of tons of dog feces. These feces would contain around 15,000,000,000 roundworm eggs.

Up to 31% of home yards and children's sand boxes in the US contain roundworm eggs.

Flushing dog's feces down the toilet is not a safe practice because the usual sewage treatments do not destroy roundworm eggs.

Infected puppies start shedding roundworm eggs at three weeks of age. They can be infected by their mother's milk.

ROUNDWORMS

The roundworms that infect dogs are known scientifically as *Toxocara canis*. They live in the dog's intestines and shed eggs continually. It has been estimated that a dog produces about 6 or more ounces of feces every day. Each ounce of feces averages hundreds of thousands of roundworm eggs. There are no known areas in which dogs roam that do not contain roundworm eggs. The greatest danger of roundworms is that they infect people, too! It is wise to have your dog tested regularly for roundworms.

In young puppies, roundworms cause bloated bellies, diarrhea, coughing and vomiting, and are transmitted from the dam (through blood or milk). Affected puppies will not appear as animated as normal puppies. The worms appear spaghetti-like, measuring as long as 6 inches. Adult dogs can acquire roundworms through coprophagia (eating contaminated feces) or by killing rodents that carry roundworms.

Roundworm infection can kill puppies and cause severe problems in adults, as the hatched larvae travel to the lungs and trachea through the bloodstream. Cleanliness is the best preventative for roundworms. Always pick up after your dog and dispose of feces in appropriate receptacles.

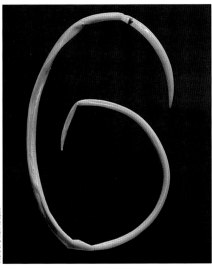

PHOTO BY DWIGHT R. KUHN.

HOOKWORMS

In the United States, dog owners have to be concerned about four different species of hookworm, the most common and most serious of which is *Ancylostoma caninum,* which prefers warm climates. The others are *Ancylostoma braziliense, Ancylostoma tubaeforme* and *Uncinaria stenocephala,* the latter of which is a concern to dogs living in the Northern US and Canada, as this species prefers cold climates. Hookworms are dangerous to humans as well as to dogs and cats, and can be the cause of severe anemia due to iron deficiency. The worm uses its teeth to attach itself to the dog's intestines and changes the site of its attachment about six times per day. Each time the worm repositions itself, the dog loses blood and can become anemic. *Ancylostoma caninum* is the most likely of the four species to cause anemia in the dog.

Symptoms of hookworm infection include dark stools, weight loss, general weakness, pale coloration and anemia, as well as possible skin problems. Fortunately, hookworms are easily purged from the affected dog with a number of medications that have proven effective. Discuss these with your veterinarian. Most heartworm preventatives include a hookworm insecticide as well.

Owners also must be aware that hookworms can infect humans, who can acquire the larvae through exposure to contaminated feces. Since the worms cannot complete their life cycle on a human, the worms simply infest the skin and cause irritation. This condition is known as cutaneous larva migrans syndrome. As a preventative, use disposable gloves or a "poop-scoop" to pick up your dog's droppings and prevent your dog (or neighborhood cats) from defecating in children's play areas.

The hookworm, *Ancylostoma caninum.*

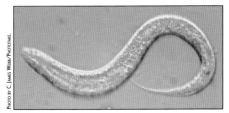

PHOTO BY C. JAMES WEBB/PHOTOTAKE.

The infective stage of the hookworm larva.

TAPEWORMS

Humans, rats, squirrels, foxes, coyotes, wolves and domestic dogs are all susceptible to tapeworm infection. Except in humans, tapeworms are usually not a fatal infection. Infected individuals can harbor 1000 parasitic worms.

Tapeworms, like some other types of worm, are hermaphroditic, meaning male and female in the same worm.

If dogs eat infected rats or mice, or anything else infected with tapeworm, they get the tapeworm disease. One month after attaching to a dog's intestine, the worm starts shedding eggs. These eggs are infective immediately. Infective eggs can live for a few months without a host animal.

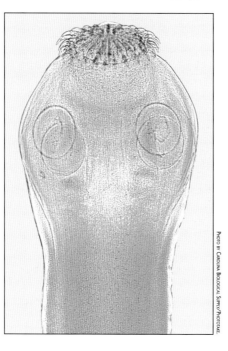

The head and rostellum (the round prominence on the scolex) of a tapeworm, which infects dogs and humans.

PHOTO BY CAROLINA BIOLOGICAL SUPPLY/PHOTOTAKE.

TAPEWORMS

There are many species of tapeworm, all of which are carried by fleas! The most common tapeworm affecting dogs is known as *Dipylidium caninum*. The dog eats the flea and starts the tapeworm cycle. Humans can also be infected with tapeworms—so don't eat fleas! Fleas are so small that your dog could pass them onto your hands, your plate or your food and thus make it possible for you to ingest a flea that is carrying tapeworm eggs.

While tapeworm infection is not life-threatening in dogs (smart parasite!), it can be the cause of a very serious liver disease for humans. About 50% of the humans infected with *Echinococcus multilocularis*, a type of tapeworm that causes alveolar hydatid, perish.

WHIPWORMS

In North America, whipworms are counted among the most common parasitic worms in dogs. The whipworm's scientific name is *Trichuris vulpis*. These worms attach themselves in the lower parts of the intestine, where they feed. Affected dogs may only experience upset tummies, colic and diarrhea. These worms, however, can live for months or years in the dog, beginning their larval stage in the small intestine, spending their adult stage in the large intestine and finally passing infective eggs through the dog's feces. The only way to detect whipworms is through a fecal examination, though this is not always foolproof. Treatment for whipworms is tricky, due to the worms' unusual life-cycle pattern, and very often dogs are reinfected due to exposure to infective eggs on the ground. The whipworm eggs can survive in the environment for as long as five years, thus cleaning up droppings in your own backyard as well as in public places is absolutely essential for sanitation purposes and the health of your dog and other dogs.

THREADWORMS

Though less common than roundworms, hookworms and those mentioned previously, threadworms concern dog owners in the Southwestern US and Gulf Coast area where the climate is hot and humid. Living in the small intestine of the dog, this worm measures a mere 2 millimeters and is round in shape. Like that of the whipworm, the threadworm's life cycle is very complex and the eggs and larvae are passed through the feces. A deadly disease in humans, *Strongyloides* readily infects people, and the handling of feces is the most common means of transmission. Threadworms are most often seen in young puppies; bloody diarrhea and pneumonia are symptoms. Sick puppies must be isolated and treated immediately; vets recommend a follow-up treatment one month later.

HEARTWORM PREVENTATIVES

There are many heartworm preventatives on the market, many of which are sold at your veterinarian's office. These products can be given daily or monthly, depending on the manufacturer's instructions. All of these preventatives contain chemical insecticides directed at killing heartworms, which leads to some controversy among dog owners. In effect, heartworm preventatives are necessary evils, though you should determine how necessary based on your pet's lifestyle. There is no doubt that heartworm is a dreadful disease that threatens the life of dogs. However, the likelihood of your dog's being bitten by an infected mosquito is slim in most places, and a mosquito-repellent (or an herbal remedy such as Wormwood or Black Walnut) is much safer for your dog and will not compromise his immune system (the way heartworm preventatives will). Should you decide to use the traditional preventative "medications," you can consider giving the pill every other or third month. Since the toxins in the pill will kill the heartworms at all stages of development, the pill would be effective in killing larvae, nymphs or adults and it takes four months for the larvae to reach the adult stage. Thus, there is no rationale to poisoning the dog's system on a monthly basis. Lastly, do not give the pill during the winter months since there are no mosquitoes around to pass on their infection, unless you live in a tropical environment.

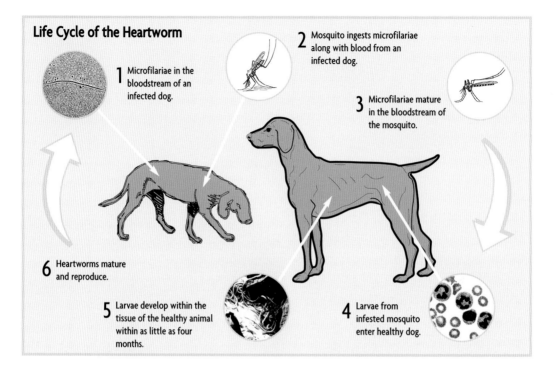

Life Cycle of the Heartworm

1 Microfilariae in the bloodstream of an infected dog.

2 Mosquito ingests microfilariae along with blood from an infected dog.

3 Microfilariae mature in the bloodstream of the mosquito.

4 Larvae from infested mosquito enter healthy dog.

5 Larvae develop within the tissue of the healthy animal within as little as four months.

6 Heartworms mature and reproduce.

HEARTWORMS

Heartworms are thin, extended worms up to 12 inches long, which live in a dog's heart and the major blood vessels surrounding it. Dogs may have up to 200 worms. Symptoms may be loss of energy, loss of appetite, coughing, the development of a pot belly and anemia.

Heartworms are transmitted by mosquitoes. The mosquito drinks the blood of an infected dog and takes in larvae with the blood. The larvae, called microfilariae, develop within the body of the mosquito and are passed on to the next dog bitten after the larvae mature. It takes two to three weeks for the larvae to develop to the infective stage within the body of the mosquito. Dogs are usually treated at about six weeks of age and maintained on a prophylactic dose given monthly.

Blood testing for heartworms is not necessarily indicative of how seriously your dog is infected. Although this is a dangerous disease, it is not easy for a dog to be infected. Discuss the various preventatives with your vet, as there are many different types now available. Together you can decide on a safe course of prevention for your dog.

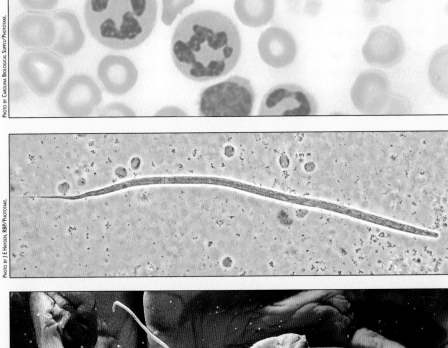

Magnified heart-worm larvae, *Diro-filaria immitis.*

Heartworm, *Diro-filaria immitis.*

The heart of a dog infected with canine heart-worm, *Dirofilaria immitis.*

HOMEOPATHY:
an alternative to conventional medicine

"Less is Most"

Using this principle, the strength of a homeopathic remedy is measured by the number of serial dilutions that were under-taken to create it. The greater the number of serial dilutions, the greater the strength of the homeopathic remedy. The potency of a remedy that has been made by making a dilution of 1 part in 100 parts (or 1/100) is 1c or 1cH. If this remedy is subjected to a series of further dilutions, each one being 1/100, a more dilute and stronger remedy is produced. If the remedy is diluted in this way six times, it is called 6c or 6cH. A dilution of 6c is 1 part in 1000,000,000,000. In general, higher potencies in more frequent doses are better for acute symptoms and lower potencies in more infrequent doses are more useful for chronic, long-standing problems.

CURING OUR DOGS NATURALLY

Holistic medicine means treating the whole animal as a unique, perfect living being. Generally, holistic treatments do not suppress the symptoms that the body naturally produces, as do most medications prescribed by conventional doctors and vets. Holistic methods seek to cure disease by regaining balance and harmony in the patient's environ-ment. Some of these methods include use of nutritional therapy, herbs, flower essences, aromather-apy, acupuncture, massage, chiro-practic and, of course the most popular holistic approach, home-opathy. Homeopathy is a theory or system of treating illness with small doses of substances which, if administered in larger quanti-ties, would produce the symptoms that the patient already has. This approach is often described as "like cures like." Although modern veterinary medicine is geared toward the "quick fix," homeopathy relies on the belief that, given the time, the body is able to heal itself and return to its natural, healthy state.

Choosing a remedy to cure a problem in our dogs is the diffi-cult part of homeopathy. Consult with your vet for a professional diagnosis of your dog's symptoms. Often these symptoms require immediate conventional care. If your vet is willing and knowledgeable, you may attempt a homeopathic remedy. Be aware that cortisone prevents homeopathic remedies from working. There are hundreds of possibilities and combinations to cure many problems in dogs, from basic physical problems such as excessive shedding, fleas or other parasites, unattractive doggy odor, bad breath, upset tummy, dry, oily or dull coat, diarrhea, obesity, ear problems or eye discharge (including tears and dry or mucusy matter) to behavioral abnormalties such as fear of loud noises, habitual licking, poor appetite, excessive barking and various phobias. From alumina to zincum metallicum, the remedies span the planet and the imagination…from flowers and weeds to chemicals, insect droppings, diesel smoke and volcanic ash.

Using "Like to Treat Like"

Unlike conventional medicines that suppress symptoms, homeopathic remedies treat illnesses with small doses of substances that, if administered in larger quantities, would produce the symptoms that the patient already has. While the same homeopathic remedy can be used to treat different symptoms in different dogs, here are some interesting remedies and their uses.

Apis Mellifica
(made from honey bee venom) can be used for allergies or to reduce swelling that occurs in acutely infected kidneys.

Diesel Smoke
can be used to help control travel sickness.

Calcarea Fluorica
(made from calcium fluoride, which helps harden bone structure) can be useful in treating hard lumps in tissues.

Natrum Muriaticum
(made from common salt, sodium chloride) is useful in treating thin, thirsty dogs.

Nitricum Acidum
(made from nitric acid) is used for symptoms you would expect to see from contact with acids such as lesions, especially where the skin joins the linings of body orifices or openings such as the lips and nostrils.

Symphytum
(made from the herb Knitbone, *Symphytum officianale*) is used to encourage bones to heal.

Urtica Urens
(made from the common stinging nettle) is used in treating painful, irritating rashes.

HOMEOPATHIC REMEDIES FOR YOUR DOG

Symptom/Ailment	Possible Remedy
ALLERGIES	Apis Mellifica 30c, Astacus Fluviatilis 6c, Pulsatilla 30c, Urtica Urens 6c
ALOPECIA	Alumina 30c, Lycopodium 30c, Sepia 30c, Thallium 6c
ANAL GLANDS (BLOCKED)	Hepar Sulphuris Calcareum 30c, Sanicula 6c, Silicea 6c
ARTHRITIS	Rhus Toxicodendron 6c, Bryonia Alba 6c
CANINE COUGH	Drosera 6c, Ipecacuanha 30c
CATARACT	Calcarea Carbonica 6c, Conium Maculatum 6c, Phosphorus 30c, Silicea 30c
CONSTIPATION	Alumina 6c, Carbo Vegetabilis 30c, Graphites 6c, Nitricum Acidum 30c, Silicea 6c
COUGHING	Aconitum Napellus 6c, Belladonna 30c, Hyoscyamus Niger 30c, Phosphorus 30c
DIARRHEA	Arsenicum Album 30c, Aconitum Napellus 6c, Chamomilla 30c, Mercurius Corrosivus 30c
DRY EYE	Zincum Metallicum 30c
EAR PROBLEMS	Aconitum Napellus 30c, Belladonna 30c, Hepar Sulphuris 30c, Tellurium 30c, Psorinum 200c
EYE PROBLEMS	Borax 6c, Aconitum Napellus 30c, Graphites 6c, Staphysagria 6c, Thuja Occidentalis 30c
GLAUCOMA	Aconitum Napellus 30c, Apis Mellifica 6c, Phosphorus 30c
HEAT STROKE	Belladonna 30c, Gelsemium Sempervirens 30c, Sulphur 30c
HICCOUGHS	Cinchona Deficinalis 6c
HIP DYSPLASIA	Colocynthis 6c, Rhus Toxicodendron 6c, Bryonia Alba 6c
INCONTINENCE	Argentum Nitricum 6c, Causticum 30c, Conium Maculatum 30c, Pulsatilla 30c, Sepia 30c
INSECT BITES	Apis Mellifica 30c, Cantharis 30c, Hypericum Perforatum 6c, Urtica Urens 30c
ITCHING	Alumina 30c, Arsenicum Album 30c, Carbo Vegetabilis 30c, Hypericum Perforatum 6c, Mezerium 6c, Sulphur 30c
MASTITIS	Apis Mellifica 30c, Belladonna 30c, Urtica Urens 1m
MOTION SICKNESS	Cocculus 6c, Petroleum 6c
PATELLAR LUXATION	Gelsemium Sempervirens 6c, Rhus Toxicodendron 6c
PENIS PROBLEMS	Aconitum Napellus 30c, Hepar Sulphuris Calcareum 30c, Pulsatilla 30c, Thuja Occidentalis 6c
PUPPY TEETHING	Calcarea Carbonica 6c, Chamomilla 6c, Phytolacca 6c

CDS
COGNITIVE DYSFUNCTION SYNDROME
"Old-Dog Syndrome"

SYMPTOMS OF CDS

There are many ways to evaluate old-dog syndrome. Veterinarians have defined CDS (cognitive dysfunction syndrome) as the gradual deterioration of cognitive abilities. These are indicated by changes in the dog's behavior. When a dog changes his routine response, and maladies have been eliminated as the cause of these behavioral changes, then CDS is the usual diagnosis.

More than half the dogs over eight years old suffer from some form of CDS. The older the dog, the more chance he has of suffering from CDS. In humans, doctors often dismiss the CDS behavioral changes as part of "winding down."

There are four major signs of CDS: frequent housebreaking accidents inside the home, sleeping much more or much less than normal, acting confused and failing to respond to social stimuli.

FREQUENT HOUSEBREAKING ACCIDENTS
- *Urinates in the house.*
- *Defecates in the house.*
- *Doesn't signal that he wants to go out.*

SLEEP PATTERNS
- *Moves much more slowly.*
- *Sleeps more than normal during the day.*
- *Sleeps less during the night.*

CONFUSION
- *Goes outside and just stands there.*
- *Appears confused with a faraway look in his eyes.*
- *Hides more often.*
- *Doesn't recognize friends.*
- *Doesn't come when called.*
- *Walks around listlessly and without a destination goal.*

FAILURE TO RESPOND TO SOCIAL STIMULI
- *Comes to people less frequently, whether called or not.*
- *Doesn't tolerate petting for more than a short time.*
- *Doesn't come to the door when you return home from work.*

The author judging a Maltese puppy. Maltese, like other small breeds, stand on a table to be examined by the conformation judge.

SHOWING YOUR
MALTESE

When you purchase your Maltese, you will make it clear to the breeder whether you want one just as a lovable companion and pet, or if you hope to be buying a Maltese with show prospects. No reputable breeder will sell you a young puppy and tell you that he is *definitely* of show quality, for so much can go wrong during the early months of a puppy's development. If you plan to show, what you will hopefully have acquired is a puppy with "show potential."

To the novice, exhibiting a Maltese in the show ring may look easy, but it takes a lot of hard work and devotion to do top winning at a show such as the prestigious Westminster Kennel Club dog show, not to mention a little luck too!

The first concept that the canine novice learns when watching a dog show is that each dog first competes against members of his own breed. Once the judge has selected the best member of each breed (Best of Breed), that chosen dog will compete with other Best of Breed dogs in his group. Finally, the dogs chosen first in each group will compete for Best in Show.

The second concept that you must understand is that the dogs are not actually compared against one another. The judge compares each dog against his breed standard, the adopted word depiction of the ideal specimen that is approved by the American Kennel Club (AKC). While some early breed standards were indeed based on specific dogs that were famous or popular, many dedicated enthusiasts say that a perfect specimen, as described in the standard, has never walked into a show ring, has never been bred and, to the woe of dog breeders around the globe, does not exist. Breeders attempt to get as close to this ideal as possible with every litter, but theoretically the "perfect" dog is so elusive that it is impossible. (And if the "perfect" dog were born, breeders and judges would never agree that it was indeed "perfect.")

If you are interested in exploring the world of dog showing, your best bet is to join your local breed club or the national parent club, which is the Maltese Club of America. These clubs often host both regional and national specialties, shows only for Maltese, which can include conformation as well as obedience and agility trials. Even if you have no intention of competing with your Maltese, a specialty is like a festival for lovers of the breed who congregate to share their favorite topic: Maltese! Clubs also send out newsletters, and some organize training days and seminars in order that people may learn more about their chosen breed. To locate the breed club closest to you, contact the American Kennel Club, which furnishes the rules and regulations for all of these events plus general dog registration and other basic requirements of dog ownership.

The American Kennel Club offers three kinds of conformation shows: an all-breed show (for all AKC-recognized breeds), a specialty show (for one breed only, usually sponsored by the parent club) and a Group show (for all breeds in the Group).

For a dog to become an AKC champion of record, the dog must accumulate 15 points at the shows from at least three different judges, including two "majors." A "major" is defined as a three-, four- or five-point win, and the number of points per win is determined on the number of dogs entered in the show on the day. Depending on the breed, the number of points that are awarded varies. In a breed as popular as the Maltese, more dogs are needed to rack up the points. At any dog show, only one dog and one bitch of each breed can win points.

Dog showing does not offer "co-ed" classes. Dogs and bitches never compete against each other in the classes. Non-champion dogs are called "class dogs" because they compete in one of five classes. A dog is entered in a particular class depending on his age and previous show wins. To begin, there is the Puppy Class (for 6- to 9-month-olds and for 9- to 12-month-olds); this class is followed by the Novice Class (for dogs that have not won any first prizes except in the Puppy Class or three first prizes in the Novice Class and have not accumulated any points toward their champion title); the Bred-by-Exhibitor Class (for dogs handled by their breeders or handled by one of the breeder's immediate family); the American-bred Class (for dogs bred in the US!); and the Open Class (for any dog that is not a champion).

The judge at the show begins judging the Puppy Class, first dogs and then bitches, and proceeds through the classes. The judge places his winners first through fourth in each class. In the Winners Class, the first-place winners of each class compete with one another to determine Winners Dog and Winners Bitch. The judge also places a Reserve Winners Dog and Reserve Winners Bitch, which could be awarded the points in the case of a disqualification. The Winners Dog and Winners Bitch, the two that are awarded the points for the breed, then compete with any champions of record entered in the show. The judge reviews the Winners Dog, Winners Bitch and all the other champions to select his Best of Breed. The Best of Winners is selected between the Winners Dog and Winners Bitch. Were one of these two to be selected Best of Breed, he or she would automatically be named Best of Winners as well. Finally the judge selects his Best of Opposite Sex to the Best of Breed winner.

At a Group show or all-breed show, the Best of Breed winners

Dog shows are entertaining and educational, as well as enjoyable social events.

Winning a presti-
gious Group in the
UK, this Maltese
typifies a
"perfect" British
show dog.

from each breed then compete for Group One through Group Four. The judge compares each Best of Breed to his breed standard, and the dog that most closely lives up to the ideal for his breed is selected as Group One. Finally, all seven group winners (from the Toy Group, Sporting Group, Hound Group, etc.) compete for Best in Show.

To find out about dog shows in your area, you can subscribe to the American Kennel Club's monthly magazine, the *American Kennel Gazette* and the accompanying *Events Calendar*. You can also look in your local newspaper for advertisements for dog shows in your area or go on the Internet to the AKC's website, www.akc.org.

ENTERING A DOG SHOW
If your Maltese is six months of age or older and registered with the AKC, you can enter him in a dog show where the breed is offered classes. Provided that your Maltese does not have a disqualifying fault, he can compete. Only unaltered dogs can be entered in a dog show, so if you have spayed or neutered your Maltese, your dog cannot compete in conformation shows. The reason for this is simple. Dog shows are the main forum to prove which representatives in a breed are worthy of

BECOMING A CHAMPION

An official AKC champion of record requires that a dog accumulate 15 points under three different judges, including two "majors" under different judges. Points are awarded based on the number of dogs entered into competition, varying from breed to breed and place to place. A win of three, four or five points is considered a "major." The AKC annually assigns a schedule of points to adjust the variations that accompany a breed's popularity and the population of a given area.

being bred. Only dogs that have achieved championships—the AKC "seal of approval" for quality in pure-bred dogs—should be bred. Altered dogs, however, can participate in other AKC events such as obedience trials and the Canine Good Citizen program.

Before you actually step into the ring, you would be well advised to sit back and observe the judge's ring procedure. The judge asks each handler to "stack" the dog, hopefully showing the dog off to his best advantage. The judge will observe the dog from a distance and from different angles, and approach the dog to check his teeth, overall structure, alertness and muscle tone, as well as consider how well the dog "conforms" to the standard. Most importantly, the judge will have

the exhibitor move the dog around the ring in some pattern that he should specify. Finally, the judge will give the dog one last look before moving on to the next exhibitor.

If you are not in the top four in your class at your first show, do not be discouraged. Be patient and consistent, and you may eventually find yourself in a winning line-up. Remember that the winners were once in your shoes and have devoted many hours and much money to earn the placement. If you find that your dog is losing every time and never getting a nod, it may be time to consider a different dog sport or to just enjoy your Maltese as a pet. Parent clubs offer other events, such as agility, tracking, obedience, instinct tests and more, which may be of interest to the owner of a well-trained Maltese.

OBEDIENCE TRIALS

Obedience trials in the US trace back to the early 1930s when organized obedience training was developed to demonstrate how well dog and owner could work together. The pioneers of obedience trials are Mrs. Helen Whitehouse Walker, a Standard Poodle fancier, who designed a series of exercises after the Associated Sheep, Police Army Dog Society of Great Britain, and her kennel manager, Mrs. Blanche

INFORMATION ON CLUBS

You can get information about dog shows from the national kennel clubs:

American Kennel Club
5580 Centerview Dr., Raleigh, NC 27606-3390
www.akc.org

United Kennel Club
100 E. Kilgore Road, Kalamazoo, MI 49002
www.ukcdogs.com

Canadian Kennel Club
89 Skyway Ave., Suite 100, Etobicoke, Ontario
M9W 6R4 Canada
www.ckc.ca

The Kennel Club
1-5 Clarges St., Piccadilly, London W1Y 8AB, UK
www.the-kennel-club.org.uk

Saunders. Since the early days, obedience trials have grown by leaps and bounds, and today there are over 2,000 trials held in the US every year, with more than 100,000 dogs competing. Any AKC-registered dog can enter an obedience trial, regardless of conformational disqualifications or neutering.

Obedience trials are divided into three levels of progressive difficulty. At the first level, the Novice, dogs compete for the title Companion Dog (CD); at the intermediate level, the Open, dogs compete for the title Companion Dog Excellent (CDX); and at the advanced level, Utility, dogs compete for the title Utility Dog

(UD). Classes are sub-divided into "A" (for beginners) and "B" (for more experienced handlers). A perfect score at any level is 200, and a dog must score 170 or better to earn a "leg," of which three are needed to earn the title. To earn points, the dog must score more than 50% of the available points in each exercise; the possible points range from 20 to 40.

Maltese, notably brilliant and trainable dogs, have proven superior in the obedience ring. The first Maltese to earn the CDX title was Ch. Tristan of Villa Malta, bred by Dr. and Mrs. Vincenzo Calveresi, and the first Maltese to win the UD title was Luce's Miss Lucy of Villa Malta, owned by B. Carlquist. A "High in Trial" award was first won by Muff of Buckeye Circle, UD.

Once a dog has earned the UD title, he can compete with other proven obedience dogs for the coveted title of Utility Dog Excellent (UDX), which requires that the dog win "legs" in ten shows. Utility Dogs who earn "legs" in Open B and Utility B earn points toward their Obedience Trial Champion title. In 1977, the title Obedience Trial Champion (OTCh.) was established by the AKC. To become an OTCh., a dog needs to earn 100 points, which requires three first places in Open B and Utility under three different judges.

The Grand Prix of obedience trials, the AKC National Obedience Invitational gives qualifying Utility Dogs the chance to win the newest and highest title: National Obedience Champion (NOC). Only the top 25 ranked obedience dogs, plus any dog ranked in the top 3 in his breed, are allowed to compete.

TRACKING

Any dog is capable of tracking, using his nose to follow a trail. Tracking tests are exciting and competitive ways to test your Maltese's inherent scenting ability. The AKC started tracking tests in 1937, when the first AKC-licensed test took place as part of the Utility level at an obedience trial. Ten years later in 1947, the AKC offered the first title, Tracking Dog (TD). It was not until 1980 that the AKC added the Tracking Dog Excellent title (TDX), which was followed by the Versatile Surface Tracking title (VST) in 1995. The title Champion Tracker (CT) is awarded to a dog who has earned all three titles. The first Maltese to win the TD and UDX titles was the famous multi-titled Joy's Mr. Feather, Am.

Consider a show-handling class to familiarize yourself with show procedures and to learn how to train your Maltese for the show ring.

AMERICAN KENNEL CLUB TITLES

The AKC offers over 40 different titles to dogs in competition. Depending on the events that your dog can enter, different titles apply. Some titles can be applied as prefixes, meaning that they are placed before the dog's name (e.g., Ch. King of the Road) and others are used as suffixes, placed after the dog's name (e.g., King of the Road, CD).

These titles are used as prefixes:

Conformation Dog Shows
- Ch. (Champion)

Obedience Trials
- NOC (National Obedience Champion)
- OTCH (Obedience Trial Champion)
- VCCH (Versatile Companion Champion)

Tracking Tests
- CT (Champion Tracker)

Agility Trials
- MACH (Master Agility Champion)
- MACH2, MACH3, MACH4, etc.

Field Trials
- FC (Field Champion)
- AFC (Amateur Field Champion)
- NFC (National Field Champion)
- NAFC (National Amateur Field Champion)
- NOGDC (National Open Gun Dog Champion)
- AKC GDSC (AKC Gun Dog Stake Champion)
- AKC RGDSC (AKC Retrieving Gun Dog Stake Champion)

Herding Trials
- HC (Herding Champion)

Dual
- DC (Dual Champion — Ch. and FC)

Triple
- TC (Triple Champion — Ch., FC and OTCH)

Coonhounds
- NCH (Nite Champion)
- GNCH (Grand Nite Champion)
- SHNCH (Senior Grand Nite Champion)
- GCH (Senior Champion)
- SGCH (Senior Grand Champion)
- GFC (Grand Field Champion)
- SGFC (Senior Grand Field Champion)
- WCH (Water Race Champion)
- GWCH (Water Race Grand Champion)
- SGWCH (Senior Grand Water Race Champion)

These titles are used as suffixes:

Obedience
- CD (Companion Dog)
- CDX (Companion Dog Excellent)
- UD (Utility Dog)
- UDX (Utility Dog Excellent)
- VCD1 (Versatile Companion Dog 1)
- VCD2 (Versatile Companion Dog 2)
- VCD3 (Versatile Companion Dog 3)
- VCD4 (Versatile Companion Dog 4)

Tracking Tests
- TD (Tracking Dog)
- TDX (Tracking Dog Excellent)
- VST (Variable Surface Tracker)

Agility Trials
- NA (Novice Agility)
- OA (Open Agility)
- AX (Agility Excellent)
- MX (Master Agility Excellent)
- NAJ (Novice Jumpers with weaves)
- OAJ (Open Jumpers with weaves)
- AXJ (Excellent Jumpers with weaves)
- MXJ (Master Excellent Jumpers with weaves)

Hunting Tests
- JH (Junior Hunter)
- SH (Senior Hunter)
- MH (Master Hunter)

Herding Tests
- HT (Herding Tested)
- PT (Pre-Trial Tested)
- HS (Herding Started)
- HI (Herding Intermediate)
- HX (Herding Excellent)

Lure Coursing
- JC (Junior Courser)
- SC (Senior Courser)
- MC (Master Courser)

Earthdog
- JE (Junior Earthdog)
- SE (Senior Earthdog)
- ME (Master Earthdog)

Lure Coursing
- JC (Junior Courser)
- SC (Senior Courser)
- MC (Master Courser)

UDT, Can. CDX, TDX, owned by C. Kollander.

In the beginning level of tracking, the owner follows the dog through a field on a long lead. To earn the TD title, the dog must follow a track laid by a human 30 to 120 minutes prior. The track is about 500 yards with up to five directional changes. The TDX requires that the dog follow a track that is three to five hours old over a course up to 1,000 yards with up to seven directional changes. The VST requires that the dog follow a track up to five hours old through an urban setting.

AGILITY TRIALS

Having had its origins in the UK back in 1977, AKC agility had its official beginning in the US in August 1994, when the first licensed agility trials were held. The AKC allows all registered breeds (including Miscellaneous Class breeds) to participate, providing the dog is 12 months of age or older. Agility is designed so that the handler demonstrates how well the dog can work at his side. The handler directs his dog over an obstacle course that includes jumps as well as tires, the dog walk, weave poles, pipe tunnels, collapsed tunnels, etc. While working his way through the course, the dog must keep one eye and ear on the handler and the rest of his body on the course.

The handler gives verbal and hand signals to guide the dog through the course.

The first organization to promote agility trials in the US was the United States Dog Agility Association, Inc. (USDAA), which was established in 1986 and spawned numerous member clubs around the country. Both the USDAA and the AKC offer titles to winning dogs. Three titles are available through the USDAA: Agility Dog (AD), Advanced Agility Dog (AAD) and Master Agility Dog (MAD). The AKC offers Novice Agility (NA), Open Agility (OA), Agility Excellent (AX) and Master Agility Excellent (MX). Beyond these four AKC titles, dogs can win additional ones in "jumper" classes, Jumpers with Weave Novice (NAJ), Open (OAJ) and Excellent (MXJ), which lead to the ultimate title(s): MACH, Master Agility Champion. Dogs can continue to add number designations to the MACH titles, indicating how many times the dog has met the MACH requirements, such as MACH1, MACH2, etc.

Agility is great fun for dog and owner with many rewards for everyone involved. Interested owners should join a training club that has obstacles and experienced agility handlers who can introduce you and your dog to the "ropes" (and tires, tunnels, etc.).

INDEX

My Maltese

PUT YOUR PUPPY'S FIRST PICTURE HERE

Dog's Name _____

Date _____ Photographer _____